One Book, One Message, One Spirit

One Book, One Message, One Spirit

Defending the Unity of Scripture

BRIAN T. WINGARD

WIPF & STOCK · Eugene, Oregon

ONE BOOK, ONE MESSAGE, ONE SPIRIT
Defending the Unity of Scripture

Wipf & Stock
An Imprint of Wipf and Stock Publishers
199 W. 8th Ave., Suite 3
Eugene, OR 97401

www.wipfandstock.com

PAPERBACK ISBN: 979-8-3852-5690-7
HARDCOVER ISBN: 979-8-3852-5691-4
EBOOK ISBN: 979-8-3852-5692-1

VERSION NUMBER 05/04/26

Unless otherwise noted, all Scripture quotations are the author's own translation.

This book is lovingly dedicated to my wife, Dorothy Brower Wingard, who has encouraged me throughout the writing and who is, apart from my salvation, the most precious gift of God I have ever received.

Contents

Preface

The Unity of Scripture and the Unity of Humanity

We live in an age of contradictions. On the one hand, tolerance is demanded of everyone. On the other hand, one segment or another of society is told that it can never be tolerated. At one time science was held up as the unassailable purveyor of truth, but now we are told that there is no such thing as objective and universal truth.

No institution has been attacked more regarding the violation of these "norms" than the Bible-believing Christian church. The church is accused of intolerance, but its message that no category or people group is excluded from the grace of the gospel is also repudiated by the world. The Bible-believing church is charged with rejecting scientific truth, but the world meets the Bible's truth claims with the mocking echo of Pilate: "What is truth?" (John 18:38).

This work is a defense of the overarching unity of Scripture. The outworking of the issues involved in the contradictions above touches the substance of the unity of Scripture and the solidarity of the human race.

Due to the ancient character of the biblical script, our culture convinces itself that the Bible is irrelevant to the complexities of postmodern life. Modernity and postmodernity deny that any document addressing an ancient culture can have anything to say about the culture of the present epoch. They cry, "We have gotten beyond all that!" There is another charge leveled apart from the antiquity of the texts. It is alleged that the Bible has its internal irrelevancies because of the various times and diverse cultures that came and went during the fifteen hundred years of its composition. Worldly wisdom says that the men and women of these various epochs and cultures would be strangers to one another and certainly strangers to people today. What relevance can words addressed to them have to us?

In addition to these issues, a theory of race has emerged that suggests that the division of the races of mankind is not to be decried but enforced. The only difference between old-fashioned racism and critical race theory is that the order in which the races are to be viewed and treated is inverted. Thus, social justice is defined not in terms of racial equality but by adjusting the demerits of inequality in the reverse direction. Therefore, statements about the equality of the races are condemned as racist because they do not give priority to groups that are considered historically underprivileged.

Biblical Christianity sees a unity in humanity based upon the teaching that all human beings are created in the image of God. Human worth is intrinsic based upon a common creation. It is not based upon those attributes that differentiate humanity.

In the title of this preface, I have used the phrase "the unity of humanity" rather than "the unity of the race" because the word *race* has become charged with passion from all sides. As I stated above, the only division of humanity that Scripture knows is a division based upon God's unmerited grace through Jesus Christ. This division is not based upon distinctions inherent to any group or class. No category of race, ethnicity, or moral superiority characterizes those who have received God's grace.

Both old-fashioned racism and contemporary critical race theory deny this truth. The Bible, nevertheless, holds out the glorious consummation of all time, when a "multitude which no man can number" will be drawn from "all tribes and peoples and tongues" surrounding the throne of God in praise and worship (Rev 7:9 ASV).

However, what if the image of this multitude is only one view of one document in a book made up of sixty-six dissimilar documents coming from a wide range of disparate time frames? Does that cast doubt upon the reality of this future vision? This work is an attempt to show that the overarching unity of Scripture, despite the diversity, provides the answer to these questions.

If we believe in the overall unity of Scripture, we must reject the evolutionary view of the Bible's development. We must also carefully scrutinize the interpretive methods of even orthodox scholars; they may be affected by a culture that rejects the relevance of the Scriptures because of their ancient and allegedly primitive character.

Preface

I, the author, spent over two decades involved in theological education in various locations in Africa. In that context, I was ever aware of the gulf that existed between my students and me. Despite these differences, I was also aware that, foundationally, we share a common humanity and possess common needs, the chief need of mankind being the grace of God through Jesus Christ.

I attempted to impress this upon my students: that in the sight of God, we are far more alike than different. This was an essential emphasis in Africa because of the presence of views that attempted to divide mankind and different parts of God's word. For example, in the sphere of global Christianity, the view that one has of the Bible and its teaching will differ as individuals from different classes and cultures enter the Bible at different points. This would mean that a white man who enters the Bible at the Pauline Epistles will have a very different view than an African or African American who enters the Bible in the book of Exodus. However, to repeat such views divides mankind and destroys the unity of Scripture in its one message to mankind.

I am convinced that in the Holy Scriptures, humankind has been given one book with one message, through the inspiration of one Spirit, in every portion. The defense of the unity of the Bible is one of the weapons the church of Jesus Christ can use to confront a culture that denies both the relevancy of the Bible and the solidarity of the human race. It is a concept that upholds the truth that humankind, in all its diversity, is at the bottom one race—the human race—which needs to hear the same message that the same Creator speaks to his creatures.[1]

1. There are other movements in our day that assail the unity of the Bible and humanity in addition to the ones mentioned in this preface. One such movement is the position held by many of the faculty members of Westminster Theological Seminary in Escondido, California. This is known as republication, teaching that the Mosaic economy is in some sense a republication of the covenant of works that existed at creation with Adam and Eve, our first parents. This is by no means as dangerous as the issues mentioned above. Nonetheless, this view does appear to suggest that there was a significant period after the fall that one segment of humanity—that is, Israel as a nation—dwelt with God in a manner that is, in some respects, significantly different than is the case with New Testament believers. If extreme care is not exercised by the proponents of this view, the idea of a unified message of the Bible to all humanity of all times and cultures may be lost. See Estelle et al., *Law Is Not*, and Elam et al., *Merit and Moses*.

Acknowledgments

I would like to acknowledge the assistance of two ladies who helped me with the preliminary task of editing. They are Mrs. Carol Brabo and Mrs. Elisabeth Bloecle; without their help the book would never have been ready for press.

Scripture Abbreviations

Old Testament

Gen	Genesis
Exod	Exodus
Lev	Leviticus
Num	Numbers
Deut	Deuteronomy
Josh	Joshua
Judg	Judges
Ruth	
1–2 Sam	1–2 Samuel
1–2 Kgs	1–2 Kings
1–2 Chr	1–2 Chronicles
Ezra	
Neh	Nehemiah
Esth	Esther
Job	
Ps (pl. Pss)	Psalm(s)
Prov	Proverbs
Eccl	Ecclesiastes
Song	Song of Solomon
Isa	Isaiah

Jer	Jeremiah
Lam	Lamentations
Ezek	Ezekiel
Dan	Daniel
Hos	Hosea
Joel	
Amos	
Obad	Obadiah
Jonah	
Mic	Micah
Nah	Nahum
Hab	Habakkuk
Zeph	Zephaniah
Hag	Haggai
Zech	Zechariah
Mal	Malachi

New Testament

Matt	Matthew
Mark	
Luke	
John	
Acts	
Rom	Romans
1–2 Cor	1–2 Corinthians
Gal	Galatians
Eph	Ephesians
Phil	Philippians

Col	Colossians
1–2 Thess	1–2 Thessalonians
1–2 Tim	1–2 Timothy
Titus	
Phlm	Philemon
Heb	Hebrews
Jas	James
1–2 Pet	1–2 Peter
1–3 John	
Jude	
Rev	Revelation

1

The Danger of the Loss of the Unity of Scripture in the Interpretive Task

The Harmonistic Method

Writing in 1943 in the preface to his work *The Five Books of Moses*, O. T. Allis said,

> The time-honored method of interpreting Scripture is the harmonistic method. This means that if the Bible is the Word of God, we are entitled to expect it to be both true and self-consistent. Consequently, Scripture is to be interpreted in the light of Scripture toward the exhibition and establishment of its harmony and unity. The higher criticism, on the other hand, begins with variations of differences, the variations in the use of the divine names in Genesis; and it gradually developed into a quest of differences. Scripture has been pitted against Scripture. Variations, however trivial and microscopic, have been magnified into contradictions. The result has been that the Bible instead of being regarded as remarkable for its unity and harmony has become in the hands of the critics a collection of writings, characterized by a diversity of viewpoints, by discord and contradiction. Such a result is destructive of its divine authority. In fact, it tends to deprive it of any authority at all. Conflicting evidence has little if any value.[1]

His book was an attack upon the so-called documentary and developmental hypotheses, which were the result of subjecting the Pentateuch to the

1. Allis, *Books of Moses*, vi–vii.

findings of higher criticism, specifically source criticism and form criticism. Allis knew the higher critics would evaluate what he called the harmonistic method as being unscientific and unscholarly.[2]

Eighty-plus years later, the phrase "harmonistic method" may have a negative ring to it in the eyes of higher critics and among many who count themselves conservative, Reformed, and Bible-believing. In our theological training, many of us learned that harmonization was wrong, or at least questionable, as a method of dealing with Scripture's linguistic variations. Scholars of all stripes still maintain that harmonization characterizes the ascendency of blind fideism over serious and scientific scholarship.

The trouble with this assessment is that it ignores the fact that the work that Allis claimed to be in the time-honored tradition of the harmonistic method proves to be a work of painstaking scholarship. It embraced Allis's minute analysis of the text and a thorough knowledge of his adversaries' position. We note that the adversaries conflicted with one another as they also differed from Allis's view of the Mosaic authorship and unity of the Torah.

I do not intend to give a treatise on the value of harmonization, though such a work would be valuable. Instead, I wish to examine the loss of the concept of the unity of Scripture among biblical scholars, whether professing orthodoxy or professing liberalism. This loss began in the higher-critical analysis of the Pentateuch and the erroneous finding that it was not a unified document but a composite from several sources that varied from one another, sometimes to the point of contradiction. It also had a basis in the equally mistaken finding that its composition took place according to an evolutionary view of the progress of ancient religious thought in general and the religious thought of Israel in particular.

The Shifting Stance of Orthodox Scholarship

How did the diversity of Scripture come to overwhelm its unity in the hermeneutical task? In addition, how did the humanity of the Bible come to supersede its divine character in the same pursuit? How did this come to be the case among orthodox scholars?

Before I answer these questions, it may be good to give a couple of examples of what I mean by the priority given to Scripture's diversity and

2. Allis, *Books of Moses*, 125.

humanity in orthodox and evangelical scholarship. In the study notes on Ps 16:9–11 in the *ESV Study Bible*, C. John Collins declares this:

> Peter cites 16:8–11 in his Pentecost speech (Acts 2:25), applying the verses to the resurrection of Jesus; Paul used Psalm 16:10 in his similar speech (Acts 13:35). If the apostles meant that David's words were a straight prediction of the death and resurrection of Jesus, it is difficult to know what function the psalm could have played in ancient Israel: the congregation would have scratched their heads in puzzlement every time they sang it.[3]

Dr. Collins says here that the historical time setting of Ps 16 means that the psalm singers in ancient Israel did not, *and could not*, understand it as a simple prediction of the resurrection of the Messiah.[4] It appears he does not think the apostles intended to use the psalm in this manner. Instead, he suggests that the apostles merely applied the general *hope of everlasting joy* from the psalm to Jesus and his resurrection.

The problem with this analysis is that it does not do justice to the plain sense of the apostles' words. For example, let us hear Peter in Acts 2:30–31:

> Being, therefore, a prophet, and knowing that God had sworn with an oath to him [David] that he would set one of his descendants on his throne, he foresaw and spoke about the resurrection of the Christ, that he was not abandoned to Hades, nor did his flesh see corruption. (ASV)

In what way can we interpret these words other than as a straight prediction of the resurrection of Jesus Christ? It is not the grammar, syntax, or logic of Acts that leads Dr. Collins to say what he does. Instead, the dominance of the times and culture of David's Israel for interpreting the psalm supposedly denies Peter the right to interpret that psalm as a straight prediction of the resurrection. Regardless of the plain sense of the apostle's words, they must be, according to Collins, an application that Peter made, not a prediction that David made.

The conclusion we must come to if we accept this view of the psalm is that Peter used misleading language in giving an application to (and not an interpretation of) the psalm. Or conversely, there is no absolute unity between David's words in Ps 16 and Peter's words in Acts 2.

3. Collins, *ESV Study Bible*, Ps 16:9–11 (956n5).

4. One assumes that Collins would allow the substitution of the more general term *Messiah* for Jesus Christ, for no one argues that David was familiar with the particular name of the Christ.

There is another inescapable conclusion to Collins's words. The *hope of everlasting joy* that he would see as the farthest expanse of David's language in the psalm was not based upon David's faith in the Messiah's future person and work (including the resurrection). Upon what, then, did the hope rest?

Collins wishes to grasp one horn of the dilemma, but another exegete of Ps 16 prefers to hold the other. Greg Herrick puts the matter this way in an article that presents his explanation of the psalm:

> Admittedly, this view creates some tensions in the text regarding the meaning of 2:30, 31—we now turn to examine these issues. The text seems to indicate that David spoke as a prophet concerning Christ's resurrection (2:30, 31), but in my exegesis, the sense of the passage has to be expanded in order to get fulfillment. This seems to minimize any prophetic aspect of the psalm in the OT and place the recognition of its prophetic nature in the experience of Peter.[5]

According to this writer, there is a discrepancy between Acts and Psalms. Peter says David was a prophet and spoke concerning the resurrection. Herrick says there was no "prophetic aspect of the psalm in the OT."[6] Thus, Peter's view of the psalm in the New Testament is at odds with the intention of David in the Old. Not to put too fine a point on the matter, Peter, according to Herrick, is simply either honestly mistaken as to David's speaking as a prophet, or he is being disingenuous.

Another example of this model of scholarship we find discussed in *Presence, Power, and Promise: The Role of the Spirit of God in the Old Testament*. The editors argue the Holy Spirit's revelation as a person did not occur in the Old Testament, and that all references to the Spirit of God were intended to be viewed as only a power emanating from God, who was viewed as a monad. They do not wish to say that he, the Spirit, was hidden but that he was not revealed in any manner at all. They give the following as a reason for this:

> One good reason for God not to reveal the Trinity or multiple persons in the Godhead to Old Testament Israel is that polytheism was such a significant problem during the period. Deuteronomy 6:4 "the Shema," was the backbone of Israelite theology; a "trinity" concept would have been considered polytheism at the time. Even

5. Herrick, "Use of Psalm 16:8–11."
6. Herrick, "Use of Psalm 16:8–11."

> the Jews in Jesus' day considered blasphemous his claim to be the "Son of God" (Matt 26:65; Mark 14:64; John 10:33). Celsus, the second-century Roman philosopher, claimed that Christians were not monotheists. It seems reasonable, then, that God could use the fairly broad word *rúah* to signify a power that emanates from him and displays itself in a variety of ways.[7]

Here we see an interpretation of the Old Testament's use of the phrase "the Spirit of God" that is at variance with the New Testament's use of the name of the Third Person of the blessed Trinity. This view suggests that Israel's weakness and the temptation to idolatry in its historical setting make it impossible for one to interpret "the Spirit of God" as a reference to, or even preparation for, the revelation of the triune nature of God. This perspective moves us away from the unity of the Bible.

Some may suggest that I disregard the principle of the progressive nature of God's revelation in my analysis. That is not so. The Bible was not written all at once, and this is obvious on the face of things, and I do not argue that David knew everything that Peter knew about the resurrection of Jesus Christ. Nor do I say that the saints of the Old Testament understood everything about the Trinity we read in our systematic theologies, confessions, and creeds.

However, the progressive nature of revelation is not a progression without a plan or purpose behind it. Biblical theology does not progress according to a natural mechanism of blind causality growing by a process analogous to Darwinian natural selection. The eternal God reveals himself in the Bible, and *he* knows the end from the beginning. Yes, his plan unfolds in Scripture, but it *is* a plan. The Lord is proactive according to his omniscience, not reactive to a condition that so-called chance might throw at him.

At the risk of speaking tautologically, I say that progress must progress. God gave new revelation to his people at various points and reminded them of his previous revelation. Otherwise, we do not have progress but stasis.

Biblical revelation is progressive, but the interpretation of that revelation cannot be bound absolutely to what we imagine the historical situation of the time made possible for God's people to understand. What did Abram's cultural moment equip him to know when God Almighty appeared to him and told him to get up and go from his father's house into a land that God

7. Firth and Wegner, *Presence, Power, and Promise*, 19–20.

would show him? This declaration was something new and stupendous, but Abram got up with his household and went. The pagan milieu that nurtured him did not prevent him from dealing with the revelation of God. As the Spirit of God can break the bonds of sin, he can break the bonds of culture.

When I suggest that orthodox scholars have retreated from the unity of Scripture, I realize I need to clarify what I mean. The term *Bible-believing* carries a commitment to the divine authority of the Scriptures as the inspired word of God, and I have no right to claim that any scholar that embraces that term denies its consequence. With respect to some orthodox scholarship, however, I have some questions. Are the concepts of the unity and diversity of Scripture parallel in some orthodox thought? Do they instead occupy separate categories in some orthodox thinking? Does Scripture's unity find a place in the category of systematic theology, and does the diversity of Scripture find its place in hermeneutics?

If this is the case, exegetical scholars could pursue their tasks as exegetes without considering the doctrinal commitments they sincerely hold. These scholars would put doctrinal obligations in the realm of faith and devotion, and exegesis in the field of scholarly endeavors accomplished with complete objectivity. The exegete can, and ought to, insist that the systematic theologian does his work in the light of exegetical concerns. Still, he may shun the notion that he ought to do his exegesis with an eye to doctrinal matters as well.

Exegetes of all stripes tend to believe the interpretation of specific texts of Scripture cannot rise higher than the knowledge possessed by the cultural setting of the writer and his audience. However, this practice not only prioritizes Scripture's diversity as texts from one epoch are set against texts from a different epoch, but it also prioritizes its humanity rather than its divinity. As mentioned above, orthodox scholars exegete using their ideas of the progressive nature of revelation. Other scholars acknowledge the Holy Spirit's divine inspiration on the writers, but with the limitations, if not the sins and errors, of their humanity. These seemingly contradictory understandings were the hallmark of neoorthodoxy arising from the writings of Karl Barth. A more contemporary expression of the dichotomy we can find in the writings of Peter Enns.[8]

How did this view of the priority of the human perspective become the consensus (minus perhaps sins and errors) even in Bible-believing scholarship? I suggest that *part* of the reason is a forgetfulness of the assumptions

8. Enns, "Apostolic Hermeneutics," 263–87.

upon which unbelievers wholly erect their scholarship (i.e., that the Bible is a thoroughly human work containing only human authority, and, at most, God uses it despite its flaws to promote some kind of religious sensibility). This forgetfulness led to the desire to give the liberals their due. This desire they put into practice by avoiding harmonization and dealing with alleged discrepancies in another manner (e.g., suggestions of the corruption of the text, redefinition of terms, etc.).

Such a practice might arise from the perception that scholarship is a great search for truth in which scholars of every stripe participate. Suspicion of the motives of others, even those disagreeing in skeptical directions, supposedly has no place in such a grand endeavor. This kind of scholarship they characterized as an objective pursuit that is unfriendly to presuppositions based on faith commitment. Therefore, any opinion rising out of this pursuit *must* receive the hearing it deserves. One may weigh it in the balance and find it wanting, but never should it be rejected unceremoniously.

We can partially understand this manner of thinking by looking at history. Orthodox scholars writing a century ago in the face of higher criticism found dismissal of their opinions the norm among their higher-critical opponents. Our generation of conservative scholars continued to believe that we should give those differing from us the courtesy that their fathers denied to ours.

However laudable this belief might be, I must question it. It is false that one can do scholarship without assumptions or presuppositions, and believing scholarship has no connection to unbelieving scholarship in the one great search for the truth. False assumptions will produce fallacious opinions. Skeptical scholarship actually flees from the truth since Jesus tells us, "Your word is truth" (John 17:17b ESV). We would do well to consider the words of Donald Fairbairn:

> Modern exegesis as a whole, with its almost fanatical commitment to each text and its exhaustive probing of all possible backgrounds to that text, is wedded to a view of reality in which the Bible is not the self-revelation of God, is not trustworthy, and is not seen as a unity. To put it another way, the painful search for "objective" methods of exegesis in the modern world may, in reality, be an attempt to discover a foundation for truth outside of the Bible itself, since the theological conviction that God has revealed himself to humanity in the words of Scripture is deemed to be either false or irrelevant.[9]

9. Fairbairn, "Patristic Exegesis," 13.

Orthodox scholars that have adopted something of this objective method do not see themselves as denying God's self-revelation. I maintain, however, that in their adoption of an objective method, they have, perhaps unwittingly, adopted a liberal assumption. This assumption arises in liberalism as a result of presuppositions that the orthodox do not share. By adopting this assumption, the conservative can sincerely hold to the inspiration and authority of Scripture but pursue a methodology in his task that is hostile to that commitment.

BACK TO THE PENTATEUCH

The quotation from O. T. Allis that opened this chapter is admittedly dated. The controversy over the documentary hypothesis of the Pentateuch no longer holds the attention of contemporary scholars. Scholars of every type have found fault with the documentary hypothesis as being far too complex and self-contradictory. This critique does not mean that Mosaic authorship has triumphed, or that the unity of Scripture as God's self-revelation has been maintained. Instead, many liberal critics now argue that the entire work is a composition of the fifth century BC. From the orthodox point of view, it is not clear that this is an improvement over the theories of Graf-Wellhausen that Allis criticized.

Why should this be so? I believe that it is because, although contemporary liberal critics have rejected the documentary and developmental hypotheses, which allegedly disproved the Mosaic authorship of the Pentateuch, they continue to view its non-Mosaic authorship as the assured position of scholarly opinion. In other words, they reject the *proof* but maintain that the conclusion must stand.

Unfortunately, unbelieving scholars will defend unbelief by fair or foul means. More troubling is the fact that some evangelical scholars adopt this view, at least regarding the book of Deuteronomy. They do this by placing its composition in the fifth century along with Joshua through Kings.[10] Nothing is threatening about such a date for Kings since its writer may have been from that period. But why should the writer of Kings be identified with the writer of Deuteronomy, or the writers of Joshua and

10. This practice is exemplified in *Survey of the Old Testament* by Hill and Walton. It is true that Hill and Walton do not say that they embrace the so-called Deuteronomistic History view, but they give it first place and only note later that some conservative scholars continue to embrace Mosaic authorship for Deuteronomy.

Judges, for that matter?[11] This cuts the fifth book of the Law from its fellows by centuries and plays into the hands of those who question the accuracy of Deuteronomy's history.

Why is it essential to tenaciously uphold the fundamental unity, the integrity, the early date, and the fact that it came mainly from Moses's hand? The Pentateuch is where God's revelation to man begins. Here we find the narrative of the creation, fall, and the beginnings of redemption. In the Pentateuch, we meet the persons we see in our Savior's genealogy. This is a genealogy that Matthew calls in Matt 1:1 "the book of the genealogy of Jesus *Christ*, the son of David, the son of Abraham."

When unity is forgotten or moved to a separate doctrinal compartment, the Bible may appear as a jigsaw puzzle of disjointed pieces painted and fit together by the differing hands of human beings. The picture the puzzle reveals becomes nothing more than the result of how the work of the various artists *happens* to match.

Suppose we recognize that the Bible is a unity that contains diversity. In that case, it allows us to see it as a tapestry that lays out the Great Creator's plan before us, which begins in Genesis and continues through Revelation.

Christianity and History

Christianity may be considered in two different ways depending upon one's view of the book that gives it its foundation. One view sees it as arising out of genuine history and the providence of the One who founded it. The other sees it as arising from unsubstantiated legends or myths.

The former view leads to doctrines that arise from history and are founded in truth and revelation, confronting the reader with their authority. In the latter view, doctrines arising from the Bible tell one only the religious thoughts of the writers to which there is no reason to lend any credence.

According to the latter view, the Old Testament and a good portion of the New Testament are historical only because they come to us as documents of the past. The accuracy of their historical narratives is entirely in doubt. It must be evaluated based on what is known about the development of religion, especially in the ancient cultures of the Middle East. According to this view, the historical records of the Bible must be corrected when they

11. Regarding the book of Joshua, let it be said that the repeat phrase "unto this day" does not appear to fit a time frame of the exile or beyond.

appear to represent ideas developed later as thoughts set down in an earlier time.

What are some ramifications of this history-of-religions viewpoint? Let us take, for example, the Bible's condemnation of idolatry, an example of what some call *ethical monotheism*. However, say the critics, such religious thoughts were of late development, so the condemnation of the golden calves at Dan and Bethel postdated their actual existence (1 Kgs 13:1–3). This is to say nothing of the curse of Aaron's calf (Exod 32). Skeptics tell us of the impossibility of monotheism as present among the Israelites in the early period.

This postmodern view of the Bible and history leads to the belief that we need to correct the religion of the Bible in its final historical form. When one reaches this conclusion, the Bible ceases to be a standard that corrects us. Instead, this view of the later evolution of religious thought leads to the need to correct the Scriptures. This way of thinking, in effect, turns matters on their heads.

Few, if any, who regard themselves as evangelical (except as that term is used in the names of some denominations) would adopt this view of the Bible and its history. However, have they unconsciously adopted some of the assumptions of the radical critics? Why does C. John Collins question the ability of the people of God of David's day to comprehend a prediction of the resurrection of the Messiah? Could it be because he believes that the concept of resurrection was unimaginable in their epoch?

Collins's thinking may be the reason the book of Hebrews seems to be at odds with him when it speaks of Abraham sacrificing Isaac (Heb 11:17–19). Many centuries before the time of David, Abraham expected to receive his son back from the sacrifice by resurrection. Giving the Pentateuch a late date would not nullify this point unless one is willing to say that the Hebrews author was reading his faith into the breast of the patriarch so that the question of Abraham's is beside the point. Yet, if we say that the statement of Hebrews is a witness only to its writer's faith and not to Abraham's faith, then the writer's whole argument in chapter 11 falls to the ground. We must make a decision. Do we believe that New Testament writers knew what they were talking about, or do we think that they erred in their belief that the faith they proclaimed was in harmony with the teaching of the Old Testament?

A Forgotten Fact and a Question of Ignorance

Liberal scholars tell us that some matters of the faith could not be revealed to Israel in the Old Testament because they did not then possess the knowledge to make certain truths understandable, such as the resurrection. This idea leads to a question they never seem to ask: What caused Israel's ignorance? It was not simply a matter of a lack of mental ability. It may have been the result of rebellion because Israel persistently refused to learn the lessons the Lord tried to teach them so tirelessly.

The phrase "they are a stiff-necked people" is repeatedly mentioned in Exodus. As we survey Israel's and Judah's history as presented in the Old Testament, we do not find a recitation of faithfulness punctuated by brief and insignificant times of faithlessness. Instead, we see a record of apostasy punctuated by brief but significant times of commitment.

Possibly Israel did not know because they did not wish a knowledge that would judge them guilty. They did not want the knowledge that would lead them to repentance and renewal that would separate them from the sinful ways they loved.

When I imply evangelical scholars have forgotten the rebellion of Israel, I do not mean to suggest that they have forgotten this as a fact of history as they exegete the multitude of passages that present Israel's rebellion. Instead, I mean that they have yet to ask needed questions regarding the principles of interpretation they utilize.

We should ask questions such as these: Did such willful ignorance from God's people restrain the Holy Spirit's freedom to reveal himself and his will to these people? Is willful ignorance a legitimate bar to the revelation of new facets of God's plan and purpose for his people and their salvation? Did God reveal himself for that generation alone or also for their posterity? How we answer these questions will determine the priority we give to the unity or diversity of the Scriptures.

In a Historical Setting or from a Historical Setting

Prepositions have an essential part to play in many languages. If I say that I am sitting *in* a house, this is very different from saying I am sitting *on* a house. The prepositions *in* and *from* are also helpful in describing theological concepts. For example, did the writers of the Bible write *in* a particular historical setting, or did they write *from* a historical background? In other words, did their historical place reflect the place they occupied on a timeline, or did it also dictate their every action, including their inspired writing? The former understanding calls for the preposition *in* and the latter the preposition *from*.

I raise this question because some will accuse me of viewing the Bible as ahistorical. I do not deny that the writers wrote *in* a historical setting, and I also believe this knowledge will play a part in interpreting the text. If writing *from* a historical background means that they were limited in what they could write by that historical setting and all their communication was bound to that setting, then this I flatly deny.

There can be no denying that the inspired writers of Holy Writ wrote in a historical setting. We would have no Bible in our possession if this were not the case. Yet they were not slavishly bound to that setting in their writing or their thoughts as they produced their work. I can say this because they were *inspired* writers (see 2 Pet 1:21).

As we use the phrase *inspired writers*, we must emphasize the two words properly. Is the focus on *inspired* or on *writers*? Some contemporary evangelical scholars, who have adopted the so-called organic view of inspiration, emphasize the human side of the equation. It almost seems as if they believed that the only objective evidence of inspiration is the inclusion of a particular book in the canon.

However, the concept of organic inspiration does not require such a view. One of the first divines to promulgate this view of inspiration was the great seventeenth-century Puritan John Owen. He said,

> We grant also that they, the sacred writers used their own abilities of mind and understanding in the choice of words and expressions: So the Preacher "sought to find out acceptable words" (Eccles. 12:10 KJV). But the Holy Spirit, who is more intimate unto the mind and skill of men than they are themselves, did guide, act, and operate in them as if they had been spoken to them by an audible voice.[12]

Owen's view of the relationship between the human writers of Scripture and the Spirit who inspired them seems analogous to the view of the Westminster Confession. The Sovereign One, though he uses *second causes*,

12. Owen, *Holy Spirit*, 145.

also works "without, above, and against them, at his pleasure."[13] God is not bound by what binds men.

The Ultimate Origin and Completion of Scripture

When one asks when the Bible was complete, one generally receives two answers. First, one is likely to give an answer concerning the dating of the last book written in the New Testament. Or there may be a discussion of the date that the canon, as we recognize it today, was complete. When one asks about the origin of the Bible, one is likely to debate which book of the Old Testament was written first. Nevertheless, I suggest that the ultimate origin and completion of the Bible are harmonious concepts. I find the key in the adjective *ultimate*. This word points us to eternity.

In eternity the Bible was already complete and in its final form in the mind of the triune God. Therefore, the origin and completion of God's word are in eternity. I can find no better statement of this concept than one found among the papers of James Henley Thornwell. Further research suggests that the statement Thornwell copied out actually originated in the writings of William Hodge Mill:

> All the objections which have been formulated as implying any incompetence in Scripture to form the sole rule of Faith appear to me to err in this: They regard the separate books of Scripture only in their individual and isolated character and overlook them in their combined and collective capacity—the true and just point of view in which they ought ever to be considered. We must remember that these inspired authors wrote not of themselves but as the Spirit of God moved them. In order therefore to estimate aright the Providential design of the Christian Scriptures, we must consider them not merely in reference to the particular intention of the individual writers in each separate composition, but we must view them in the integrity of their first composition as they appeared in the counsels of eternity of Him to whom is known all His works from the beginning. I am fully persuaded that such a comprehensive and combined survey of the Christian Scriptures will amply convince us that they contain in themselves a summary

13 Westminster Standards, Confession of Faith, 5.3.

> of the whole body of Christian doctrine such as neither to require not to admit any extraneous additions whatsoever.[14]

This statement emphasizes "the integrity of their first composition" because God knows all of his works from the beginning. By this, Mill reminds us that the Bible is one of the works of God. Therefore, above the intention of the individual writers is the intention of God, the Holy Spirit, who inspired them.

Since the Holy Spirit inspires the Bible, one ignores this eternal standpoint of the origin and completion of Scripture at his peril. Moreover, this is a matter that ought to shape how we pursue our exegesis. We dare not relegate the concept of inspiration and the parallel concept of the unity of Scripture to the category of doctrinal theology. To do so deprives our exegesis of the eternal vantage point, which is the vantage point of "the integrity of their first composition." If I may return to the distinction between *in* and *from*, then let me say that the human writers of the Bible wrote *in* history, while the divine Author conceived it *from* eternity.

14. Mill, *Essays on the Church*, 5.

2

The Divine Purpose of the Bible

The Bible Has a Divine Purpose

If, as Mill says (as I quoted him at the end of chapter 1), the Bible has its native integrity in eternity past, then the implication is that it has a divine and eternal purpose. We do not mean that it is useless for scholars to ask what the goals of the individual writers of the books are; however, there must be an overarching purpose of Scripture in which all its constituent parts partake.

This is the sine qua non for any genuine profession of the inspiration and authority of Scripture. That does not mean that all who make such an honest confession agree concerning the Bible's purpose. Individual definitions of that purpose might differ widely as various people set forth the purpose. Nevertheless, there is no unity in the Scriptures if it has no discernible purpose.

As stated, agreeing that there is an overriding purpose is easy; coming to a consensus about the purpose's nature is harder. Some seek the briefest possible purpose statement to avoid violating the historical, societal, and cultural differences governing the individual text's interpretation. Others seek a purpose so detailed that they express some, if not all, of the subordinate goals of the Bible. Still others seek a middle ground.

There may not even be agreement about the nature of the overarching purpose and the Bible's unity. Is the purpose illustrative of the direction in which all the content of the Bible points? Similarly, is it illustrative of a common theme to which all the constituent parts give voice? Instead, does the purpose only highlight a progression of teaching, emphasizing underlying diversity rather than concealing it?[1]

Therefore, it is necessary to delve into these matters after stating that the Bible has a purpose. What is the nature of the Bible's aim, and how may it be defined?

The Nature of the Purpose

What kind of purpose does the Bible have? Is it ultimately divine or ultimately human? Is the plan intrinsic and internal to the Bible or acquired and external, imported onto the text? Is the nature of the purpose of the whole Bible consistent with the subordinate objectives found in individual books? Is the purpose of the Bible pertinent to all the readers of the Bible or only the original audience? If so, is it apropos in the same manner to all? Does the Bible's purpose deal with issues of ultimate significance or matters of relatively minor importance? The answers that we give to these questions will determine to a large degree how we will deal with Scripture.

I shall begin the discussion with the answer to the first question. The purpose of the Bible is divine. By this, I mean that it is a book that comes from God, and he is responsible for its content and its designs. Therefore, the purpose is divine, not merely that it has God as its subject matter. Scripture both originates and terminates in the Lord. The divine Being is both the subject of the Bible and its object.

Knowing that the purpose of the Bible is divine will shape our expectations when we come to it. It will lead us to expect Scripture to be consonant with the One whose purpose exists in it. God is eternal; therefore, we should expect the Bible to have an eternal perspective. God is the God of perfect moral rectitude and justice, so we expect that to be part of the perspective that meets us in Scripture. God is omniscient; thus, we expect the word of God to partake of that attribute. The Bible will come to us with the certainty of the One whose purpose controls it.

1. This third alternative may need a bit of illustration. I use *Norton's Anthology* for this purpose, an anthology of English literature that begins with *Beowulf* and continues through *The Canterbury Tales* and Shakespeare up to the modern period. There is certainly a purpose for the anthology as a whole, but it has nothing to do with a supposed common theme to the individual pieces of literature. Instead, the aim is to highlight the progressive development of English literature. No one, for example, would see a common theme in *Beowulf* and Shelley's "Ozymandias." Of course, there might be themes common to more than one of the works, but none is common to them all.

The statement from the previous chapter about the Bible having an eternal perspective is worthy of further comment. The books of the Bible were, no doubt, written in history, which causes some people to expect that the perspective that meets us in those books is merely historical. However, as mentioned, the Scriptures were written from eternity, guaranteeing that there will also be an eternal perspective.

There are practical ramifications to a divine and eternal perspective of the word of God. These consequences affect the way pastors address issues of pastoral ministry. Imagine that a pastor addresses a man who wishes to divorce his wife on other than biblical grounds. Imagine, moreover, that he argues to the pastor that the Bible written so long ago cannot presume to dictate situations in the contemporary life of which the writers of Scripture were unaware. Nevertheless, the divine and eternal perspective of the Bible gives the pastor the authority to point to the eternal Spirit, who inspired the word, and gives eternal significance and relevance to its teachings.

In the example above, knowing the omniscience of God would give the pastor practical counsel. The husband may say, "I don't care what the Bible says; I *know* that God would never want me to stay married to this woman." In this situation, the pastor can confront the man with the all-knowing Spirit, who inspired the Bible and did not allow his knowledge of this particular case to alter the regulations of biblical divorce.

If the purpose of the Bible is consistent with the perfect righteousness and truth of the God who gave it, the Christian has the armor to face the gainsayers and skeptics. Knowing that God cannot lie so that his purpose in Scripture is not deceptive defends us against the plausible arguments of unbelievers. We do not trust our reason when placed beside God's eternal truth. Likewise, we do not trust the skeptic's reasoning when placed in opposition to that same truth. Walter C. Kaiser quotes Samuel Taylor Coleridge to this effect: "When we meet an apparent error in a good author, we are to presume ourselves ignorant of his understanding until we are certain that we understand his ignorance."[2] If this is true of a mere good author, what does it say about the divine Author of the eternal word? How shall any presume to understand the ignorance of the One who possesses none?

The answer to my first question (that the purpose of the Bible is divine and not merely human) leads to the answer to the second question. The purpose of Scripture is intrinsic, not external and acquired. Suppose we focus on the human component of the individual books and limit our

2. Kaiser, *Recovering the Bible*, loc. 628 of 4925.

interest to the purpose of the writers. In that case, the idea of a purpose that is overarching will necessarily appear to be external and acquired. The recognition that the ultimate purpose of the Bible is divine and, therefore, present from the very inception of its writing allows us to accept this purpose as inherent to the Bible itself.

Suppose the overarching purpose of the Bible is inherent in it and not an external addition. In that case, we expect it to be in harmony with the subordinate purposes of the individual books written by human writers. This concept governs our handling of the text. Ideally, we would not go out of our way to pit the divine purpose against the human. By the same token, we should not attempt to resist accepting the Holy Spirit's commentary on one book of the Scriptures by another book because it conflicts with *our understanding* of the aim of the previous book.

For example, though many commentators have not done so, we should accept Paul's assertion that Hosea prophesied the inclusion of the gentiles into the church even though *it seems to us* to go contrary to Hosea's purpose (see Rom 9:25–26). Modern-day conservative scholars that have assumed a discrepancy have gotten themselves into a morass by attempting to suggest that the Holy Spirit was graciously providing Paul with an entirely different understanding of the text of Hosea from the prophet's intention. Wiser is John Calvin, who interprets Paul in complete harmony with the purpose of Hosea's prophecy:

> And this is what is chiefly included in the present prophecy: when the Jews were banished from God's family, they were thus reduced to a common class and put on a level with the Gentiles. The difference being taken away, God's mercy is now indiscriminately extended to all the Gentiles. We hence see that the prophet's prediction is fitly applied to the present subject, in which God declares that after having equalized the Jews and the Gentiles, he would gather a Church for himself from aliens so that they who were not a people would begin to be so. I will call them my people, which are not a people. This is said concerning the divorce, which God had already made with the people by depriving them of all honor so that they did not excel the other nations. Though they indeed, whom God in his eternal counsel has destined as sons to himself, are perpetually his sons. Yet, Scripture in many parts counts none to be God's children but those whose election has been proved by their calling: and hence he teaches us not to judge, much less to

> decide, respecting God's election, except as far as it manifests itself by its evidence.[3]

Calvin did not believe there was a contradiction between the purpose that the Holy Spirit enunciated through Hosea and the purpose that the same Spirit spoke through the apostle Paul. Calvin's view is consistent with the understanding that the overarching aim of the Bible is inherent in it and not imposed upon it from the outside. Why is there such a difference between Calvin and more contemporary evangelical commentators? Perhaps it is because Calvin did not begin reasoning from the standpoint that differences in language or perceived theological meaning naturally lead to the presence of discrepancy or contradiction unless proved otherwise.

Is the purpose of the Bible pertinent to all the readers of the Bible or only the original audience? Was the Bible written for us who live in the twenty-first century? How believers answer this question depends upon the definition of the phrase *written for us*. The Bible is dear to all true believers, even today, and one reason it is so special is that they find it a guide to their faith and practice. Some, however, believe that the interpretation of the biblical text, especially the prophetic, is pertinent only to original audiences. They say it applies to today's believers only by way of application.

For instance, many have a limited view of the enthronement psalms such as Ps 16, mentioned in chapter 1, and Ps 2. Some tell us that Ps 2 was initially a song in praise of David or the enthronement of another righteous king, and the writer of the psalm permitted himself to use hyperbole in speaking about the king in almost divine terms. If we follow this interpretation, we learn that these psalms are messianic only because the words are suited to Jesus the Messiah, who finally arrived upon the scene centuries later.

If this is the proper way to interpret this psalm, then it is not messianic in any sense. Commentators no longer see the psalm as preparatory for his coming but merely as a piece of writing that was appropriate when he happened to arrive. There is no prediction if the interpretation is exclusively addressed to the original audience. It becomes a matter of happy happenstance that the inflated language of the psalm suits Jesus Christ much better than it does David or another king of Israel or Judah.

I do not intend to deny the concept of typology. David, and were, to a lesser extent, other kings in the messianic genealogy, was a type of messiah. A type, however, is subservient to the antitype. It is the shadow preparing

3. Calvin, *Commentary on Romans*, 378–79.

the way for reality. This preparation is different from what the distinction of interpretation versus application implies. The interpretation is what the psalm means, and the application is how the psalm may be used. Therefore, in the hermeneutical sense, meaning is primary—not application.

How do we know that the psalm *applies* to Jesus in the final and quintessential manner? Are there others to whom the words of the psalm are also suitable? A secondary application to Jesus is unsatisfying because the words of the psalm fit Jesus so much better than they fit David. The writer of Hebrews tells us in Heb 1:5 that the declaration, "You are my Son," in Ps 2 proves Jesus Christ to be superior to the angels. If God originally spoke these words to David, do they mean that he was as superior to the angels as Jesus is?

The Christian believer needs to understand that God speaks to him or her in the Bible. The same believer must be confident that he or she is not addressed as second class. Christians need to know that they are not reading other people's mail when they pick up their Bibles to read.

The Bible itself indicates that the writers and faithful believers of past ages understood that the great promises of God did not terminate with them, nor was their ethos or life situation the primary focus of the promises.

> All these died in faith, without receiving the promises, but having seen them and having welcomed them from a distance, and having confessed that they were strangers and exiles on the earth. (Heb 11:13 NASB)

> As to this salvation, the prophets who prophesied of the grace that *would come* to you made careful searches and inquiries, seeking to know what person or time the Spirit of Christ within them was indicating as He predicted the sufferings of Christ and the glories to follow. It was revealed to them that they were not serving themselves, but you, in these things which now have been announced to you through those who preached the gospel to you by the Holy Spirit sent from heaven—things into which angels long to look. (1 Pet 1:10–12 NASB; emphasis mine)

The New Testament quotations show that the Old Testament saints and prophets knew that there was something in the future that signified something grander than the experience of their present moment. Walter Kaiser makes a very apropos statement regarding the text from 1 Peter, challenging some who have used the passage to teach that the Old Testament prophets were puzzled by any future understanding of their words:

> Nevertheless, some claim that 1 Peter 1:10–11 taught that the prophets were generally at a loss to understand their own prophecies. One must admit that, as the text teaches, the Old Testament prophets "searched intently and with the greatest care, trying to find out the time and circumstances [Greek, *eis tina e poion kairon*] to which the Spirit of Christ in them was pointing" when they received utterances. But it was only the time or the particular set of circumstances that was withheld from them, for the text of Peter claims five things the prophets realized about the revelation given to them. They knew (1) they were speaking about the Messiah, (2) the Messiah would have to suffer, (3) the Messiah would experience "glory," (4) suffering would come first and glory would follow, and (5) their words had relevancy not only for themselves but for later generations, such as the one Peter was addressing in the church.[4]

What relevancy, then, did the prophecies of the Messiah and messianic psalms have for the saints of the Old Testament? Some question whether they had any relevancy if these were straight prophecies of the Messiah, as Kaiser seems to believe that at least some were. We saw this already in the comment of C. John Collins about the apostles' use of Ps 16 in the book of Acts. If, however, in the present day, men and women can find salvation and receive comfort by looking back upon the Messiah who has come and is coming again, then what debarred the believers in the Old Testament from seeking redemption and finding comfort in the Messiah who was to come? The only alternative that appears to make sense is the suggestion that there was a different way of salvation before the Messiah's birth that had nothing to do with faith in him. I will not deal with that suggestion now since we have yet to discuss the overarching purpose of the Bible.

One question remains that I should answer about the nature of the Bible's overarching purpose. Is this purpose of ultimate significance or not? This question is a difficult one to answer since it depends to such a large degree on the definition of terms. What do I mean by the word *ultimate*, and what do I mean by *significance*? Moreover, to whom is it or is it not of utmost importance, and from what perspective can one decide this?

By *ultimate*, I mean something that gives place to nothing else. The term refers to that which is highest and without rival. By the word *significance*, I mean to include both the concepts of importance and meaning.

4. Kaiser, *Recovering the Bible*, loc. 1510 of 4925.

Answering the actual question is harder to navigate. If the glory of God is connected with the Bible's overarching purpose, and if we agree that we should do all things to God's glory (1 Cor 10:31), then the question is somewhat meaningless because all things in Scripture deal with God's glory to some extent. How, then, can we speak of something that takes precedence over all other matters? First Corinthians 10:31, however, is not the only biblical passage from which to view the question. In the same epistle, Paul says in chapter 15 that the message he delivered to the Corinthians was of "first importance" (v. 3). From that perspective, we recognize that there were different levels of significance in the apostle's teaching.

I am discussing at this point the overarching purpose of Scripture, and I do not deny subordinate objectives that individual parts of the Bible may set forth. When it concerns the overriding purpose of the Bible, I maintain that it involves matters of ultimate significance and not lesser importance.

The God of glory was under no obligation to reveal himself to humankind. His reason for doing so is supposedly related to the importance of the revelation for those receiving it. The Lord of glory does not lend himself to trivialities. Jesus said to Satan, "Man shall not live by bread alone, but by *every* word that proceeds out of the mouth of God" (Matt 4:4). If *every* word of God's mouth is that by which we *live*, then *every* word is a means of life and, therefore, essential. God's word to his people makes up their spiritual diet and provides true life.

When a Scripture passage is treated as if its true meaning and purpose are entirely bound to the concerns of an isolated epoch, then the synergistic interplay of scripture with scripture is set at risk. How could Paul write to Timothy that his knowledge of the Scriptures (*gramata*) was able to make him "wise unto salvation" (2 Tim 3:15)? Paul viewed the writings of the Old Testament as concerning salvation. Note that the verse continues to say that salvation is "through the faith in Jesus Christ" (*dia pisteous taes en Christo Yaesus*; 2 Tim 3:15). The conclusion is inescapable. *All* Scripture is to equip the "man of God" for his ministry, and this man of God is viewed as living contemporaneously with Timothy and Paul (see 2 Tim 3:15–17). Therefore, I conclude that the salvation that the scriptures of the Old Testament revealed was "through faith in Jesus Christ" and relevant to the work of the ministry in Paul's time, as well as our own.

The Identity or Content of the Divine Purpose of the Bible

At some length, I have dealt with the nature of God's purpose in the Bible. Now I ask, what *is* that purpose? What thread runs through Genesis to Revelation and encompasses all its contents? If one states the purpose in its most succinct form, it is easy to remember but also leads to possible misunderstanding. This succinct form may be stated: God's purpose in the Bible is to reveal himself to man.

If the stated purpose is left at that, the questions at the foundation of this discussion remain just that, questions. In that case, this chapter would be redundant! More ought to be said.

The expanded form of the purpose can be stated like this: *God's purpose in the Bible is to reveal himself to man to the praise of his glory in the complete salvation of his people.* The statement can be misleading if the words are not appropriately defined; it needs some unpacking. For example, one might think that the word *salvation* confines the purpose to the bare justification of believers. However, the biblical view of salvation encompasses everything from regeneration to glorification, so I have included the descriptor *complete.*

The first part of the expanded purpose says that the Lord pre-purposes to reveal himself in the Bible. God intends the Scriptures to be the means of his self-disclosure, but what does he intend to disclose? It is his person, his work, his will, and his providential dealing with his creatures.

Some may ask, Is this an authentic self-disclosure? Can he, who is "infinite, eternal and unchangeable,"[5] disclose himself in any proper manner? Can the Infinite make himself known to the finite? Can an infinite gap be closed? Many people stumble at questions such as these.

Their stumbling may be because they need to correct the perspective from which they ask the question. A finite being cannot overcome an infinite gap. An infinite being, however, *can* overcome an infinite gap. The human ability to comprehend the incomprehensible is not the issue, and the ability of the Almighty to do as he pleases is the issue.

We cannot know God as he knows himself. Only God knows God in that sense. However, this does not mean that God is unknowable. Knowledge of God can be posited in three ways. First, one may claim univocal knowledge. Univocal knowledge is a knowledge that is absolutely the same

5. Westminster Standard, Shorter Catechism, Q/A 4.

as God's knowledge in those areas where human knowledge and divine knowledge overlap. Second, one might maintain that all alleged understanding of God is equivocal. This is not to say it is false knowledge, but it would be uncertain knowledge, at best. Third, some have called human knowledge of God analogous to God's knowledge of himself. This means there is a correspondence between our knowledge of God and God's knowledge, assuming it is taken from Scripture, but it is not identical. A topographical map of the United States is analogous but not identical to the United States, even if it is created from a satellite image. Nevertheless, it is valuable, and for all intents and purposes, it gives an accurate picture of the United States.

If I am forced to choose, I must choose the third option. Yet I believe more needs to be said. The knowledge of God that one can gain from Scripture, even if correctly interpreted, is not identical to God's knowledge of himself. Still, it is the knowledge God wishes the Bible's readers to have. The trouble with my illustration of the map is that a human cartographer produces the map. To make this an accurate analogy of what takes place in Scripture, the United States would have to create the map by using the mind and hands of the cartographer as its tools. For mapmaking, the thought is ridiculous, but for the process of God's revelation of himself, it makes the point. The Bible is precisely what God wants it to be, and because he is a God of truth, there is no equivocation.

The Lord's purpose in the revelation of himself in the Bible has an end in view, and a means to accomplish that end. The goal of God's revelation in Scripture is the praise of his glory, and how to elicit that praise is the demonstration of redemption through the person and work of Jesus Christ.

What is God's glory that we are to praise? Is it not the perfection of God set before us in the pages of the Bible? The Holy One is the Being set apart from every other being. "'To whom then will you liken Me that I would be his equal?' says the Holy One" (Isa 40:25 NASB). This pronouncement is manifest in what are known as his incommunicable attributes. Still, it is also displayed in his communicable attributes since how he possesses and exercises them is unique to himself.

God's glory displayed in his perfection and holiness is not designed for mere intellectual rumination. God intends his glory to elicit our worship and praise. "Take the shoes from your feet," said the Lord to Moses when he appeared in the burning bush, "for the ground upon which you stand is holy ground" (Exod 3:5). Worship and praise are what all human beings owe to the Creator, Governor, and Redeemer.

Nevertheless, there is a supreme place where the praise of God's glory finds its center: Jesus Christ and his salvation. One uses Scripture in vain if its center is not there! "You examine the Scriptures," said Jesus to his detractors, "because you think that in them you have eternal life; and it is those *very Scriptures* that testify about Me" (John 5:39 NASB, emphasis mine). "For I determined to know nothing among you," wrote Paul to the Corinthians, "except Jesus Christ and Him crucified" (1 Cor 2:2 NASB).

Recognizing the Divine Purpose of the Bible

Some will argue that simply stating a specific purpose to the Bible does not make it so. How is it possible to recognize this purpose? A complete answer to that question would take a whole book. Nevertheless, about this subject I will briefly speak.

First, a pattern of Scripture seems to indicate that the purpose is present. This pattern begins with the way the Bible opens. Genesis's first and second chapters set up God's creation of the universe. He is the central actor, and he, not the creature, evaluates what he makes. Creation is an act of revelation, and it displays his glory. Yet very quickly, the narrative brings us to Adam's fall into sin, but it also promises that the seed of the woman will triumph over the serpent, the embodiment of Satan.

Nevertheless, the promise is not entirely fulfilled by the end of Genesis or the end of the Pentateuch. The first possible candidate to claim the promise, Cain, proves a disaster. Joseph, with whom Genesis closes, is promising in many ways as he moves near the summit of earthly power and brings a great deliverance. Yet, he dies without the fulfillment of the full promise. Moses, the central human character of the rest of the Pentateuch, shows his fallibility in the sin that keeps him from entering the land of promise, the books of the Law concluding with his death on Mount Nebo.

If the promise of Gen 3:15 concerned only one book or series of books in the canon, would it not have its fulfillment within that book or books? God promised something at the very beginning that remains unfulfilled throughout the Old Testament. It is not forgotten, for the prophets reiterate the promise. Malachi, the book at the end of the Old Testament, repeats the promise as the progressive revelation has refined it.

The New Testament begins with Matthew's statement of the identity of the Messiah in the person of Jesus. He does so by pointing to the genealogy of Christ from Abraham through David to Joseph, the husband of Mary, Jesus's mother. Thus, the New Testament presents the fulfillment of the promises of the Old.

It ends with the consummation of all history in the new heavens and the new earth. It presents Jesus Christ as the Lamb who becomes the light of the new Jerusalem, replacing that of the sun. The place of the one tree of life that God planted in the garden of Eden before the fall presents a multitude of such trees, whose leaves are "for the healing of the nations" (Rev 22:2b NASB).

In this, the purpose and balance of Scripture are given to us to see. Creation at its beginning is balanced with new creation at its end. The disastrous work of Satan in leading humanity into sin is balanced at the end by Jesus Christ casting him headlong into hell. Thus, the promise of Gen 3:15, fulfilled in the penultimate sense on the cross, is here fulfilled in the ultimate sense. We might say that the sentence pronounced upon Satan at the Savior's sacrifice is executed in the consummation. Between the beginning and end of the New Testament, there are multitudes of signs that tie the promises of the Old Testament to their fulfillment in the New.

In addition to this general pattern that points to the divine purpose of Scripture are statements concerning individual books that point to a similar purpose. Perhaps the clearest of these is found in John 20:31. John writes, "But these things are written that you might believe that Jesus is the Christ, the Son of God, and so that believing you might have life in His name."

Conclusion

There is, therefore, an overarching divine purpose in the Bible. It concerns what is of utmost importance: the revelation of God to the praise of his glory in the complete salvation of his people. Since this is the case, the unity of Scripture must be more than a matter of doctrinal confession; it should color and shape how we approach the serious study of God's word. When our eyes are on this purpose, it should cause us to examine carefully every suggestion of hermeneutical practice that seeks to minimize the unity of the Bible to maximize its diversity. The knowledge that the overarching purpose is divine should make one wary of maximizing the human composition of Scripture at the expense of the divine elements.

3

Digging Deeper

Introduction

Recognizing that there is an overarching divine purpose in the Bible assures one that the Bible has overall unity. However, I would make a mistake in attempting to make every statement of Holy Writ a direct manifestation of this purpose. Previously, I stated that the presence of an overarching purpose of Scripture does not nullify the subordinate aims of the individual writings. For example, God revealed that he would pour out his impending judgment upon the rebellious people of Judah and Jerusalem. Only the simpleminded would assert that the judgment pronounced was considered a straightforward prediction of the coming Messiah. Nevertheless, it shows the need for Messiah, and in this light, one is justified in analyzing Jeremiah's prophecy of the new covenant that God will make with his people and the new hearts that he will give them (see Jer 31:31).

The discussion of the Bible's divine purpose does not close the debate on the unity of Scripture; rather, in a sense, it opens it. In this chapter, I will discuss the rightful place that Scripture's unity should have in that divine purpose, despite the diversity in its human composition.

The Wiles of Satan

I need to begin this section with a necessary disclaimer. The title is not meant to suggest that any Bible scholar is self-consciously in league with the devil. Yet we are warned in Scripture to resist him and that he is actively engaged in opposing God and his Christ. As he was able to deceive Eve, so he can cause even earnest and sincere Christians to succumb to his devices and lies upon occasion. Therefore, the warning to resist him is as much directed to me as to others.

In suggesting that our adversary might have a part in the debate over proper biblical interpretation, I place myself under the possible charge of being supremely unscholarly. Twenty-three years of teaching in Africa, however, has taught me that the postmodern and Western denial of the reality of Satan and his fallen angelic host is a supreme example of his cunning in hiding his existence. Moreover, since Satan may play a part in both the recorded history of the Bible and the history of interpretation, it is unscholarly to ignore his influence.

"Has God really said that you shall not eat of any of the trees of the garden?" the serpent asked Eve (Gen 3:1). When Satan took Jesus to the pinnacle of the temple, he said, "Cast yourself off, for it is written, 'He shall give his angels charge concerning you, *and* upon their hands they shall bear you up, lest at any time you dash your foot against a stone'" (Matt 4:6). In both of these scenarios, the enemy attempted to abuse God's word for his ends. Do we have reason to believe that he has no stake in the discussion we are pursuing?

Who benefits when the number of so-called straight references in the Old Testament to Christ, his person, and his work is reduced to the barest minimum? Who benefits when the Holy Spirit's presence in the Old Testament is denied in favor of the presence of a vague *power* emanating from God? Who benefits when New Testament writers adducing the Old Testament texts supporting their arguments are accused of abusing the sense and intention of the Old Testament writers? Who benefits when scholars embrace a postexilic date for Deuteronomy? Who benefits when the religion of the New Testament is presented in such a way that it appears as if it has no solid foundation in the religion of the Old? Questions such as these cause this writer to hold out the possibility that subtle suggestions of Satan might infiltrate these matters.

I do not say these things to throw brickbats. Bible-believing scholars acknowledge the work of the Holy Spirit in the compiling and preserving of the Bible. His involvement in the historical understanding of the Bible is denied by none but rank unbelievers. Why is the opposition of Satan ignored in the same process? Offense to others who do not believe in Satan is a dangerous basis for ignoring a contributing factor when making an analysis. Liberal scholars tend to deny Satan's existence in their interpretive work. Bible-believing scholars ought to take care they do not ignore Satan's wiles as they pursue their work.

Jesus suggested satanic involvement played a part in the opposition he received from his adversaries. Paul reminds us that our struggle is not against mere flesh and blood but powers and principalities. Do we only struggle with them in the personal realm, or is their influence also at work in intellectual pursuits?

It would probably raise no eyebrows among evangelicals for me to suggest that Satan played a role in doctrinal heresies of the past. Why does anyone shy away from the possibility we can find his hand in errors of hermeneutical practice?

Reformed orthodoxy has rightly criticized the neo-fundamentalists for displaying anti-intellectualism in their work. Nevertheless, it is equally unwise to ignore the attempted influence of Satan or his fallen angels in the process of biblical scholarship. Our fathers in the faith, such as O. T. Allis, J. Gresham Machen, and E. J. Young, were concerned about resisting the anti-supernaturalism of the *higher critics* of their day. Is biblical supernaturalism only a matter of the formation and context of the text, or does it also involve the interpretation of the text?

The recognition of spiritual warfare in the work of *all* scholars involved in theological undertakings ought to lead us to ask questions concerning our labors. What consequences of our endeavors will occur in the hearts and minds of believers? Will it lead them to a warmer and more devoted attachment to their God and Savior, or will it lead them away from such devotion and attachment? Will the endeavor lead to a reverence for God's word, or will it lead in the opposite direction? Are the questions of intellectualism and scholasticism focusing upon the most important questions? What agenda will one's work promote, God's or Satan's?

The Solidarity of the Race

Are different human beings more alike, or are they more different? Are the similarities fundamental to their beings, or are their differences? These questions have relevance in the racially charged atmosphere of our times, but they also have relevance in the task of interpreting the Bible. Are the ethnic, historical, and cultural differences that separate us from Bible times so radical and fundamental to make it nearly impossible to understand what the biblical writers were saying to the people of their day? Is the gap between culture and centuries so vast that it is almost hopeless to cross the divide? How is one to answer these questions?

The answer one gives to the historical and cultural question will depend significantly upon the relative importance of the similarities versus the differences between men and women. I believe that my answer is eminently biblical, that there is a solidarity of the human race. Paul declared to the Athenians on Mars Hill,

> And He made from one man every nation of mankind to live on all the face of the earth, having determined their appointed times and the boundaries of their habitation, that they would seek God if perhaps they might grope for Him and find Him, though He is not far from each one of us; for in Him we live and move and exist, as even some of your own poets have said, "For we also are His children." (Acts 17:26–28 NASB)

Notice that the differences in mankind that he notes—"appointed times and the boundaries of their habitation"—are minor to the common origin. Also note their need to seek the God who is near them, and the common fatherhood of God over all. Paul thus makes his gospel appeal to them based on the solidarity of the human race. Despite mankind's differing times and boundaries of habitation, the Lord declares "to men that all *people* everywhere should repent, because he has fixed a day in which He will judge the world in righteousness through a Man whom He has appointed, having furnished proof to all men by raising Him from the dead" (Acts 17:30b–31 NASB, emphasis in the original).

The Holy Spirit in his word chose to speak to the similarities of mankind as well as their differences. The opening of the prophecy of Amos is noteworthy. There Amos declares God's judgment upon various nations with this introductory phrase each time: "For three transgressions of [the specific nation], and for four, I will not revoke its punishment" (Amos 1:3). Why should the Israel of Amos's day show interest in the judgment on Damascus, Philistia, Phoenicia, the Amorites, the Edomites, or even Judah? Amos can use these condemnations of neighboring nations and people groups as preliminary to the Lord's condemnation of Israel because of their similarities, not their differences.

What has the solidarity of the race to do with the unity of Scripture? All of the human race of all times and places has one origin in the creation of Adam and Eve. All partake of the same needs and emotions. We are all subject to the curse, and all of the race fell into sin and slavery.

These last-mentioned matters are the most critical issues to consider. If the Bible's purpose is to reveal God to mankind to the praise of his glory in the salvation of Jesus Christ, then that salvation is the same for all mankind since the fall. It will not differ from place to place, from epoch to epoch, or from culture to culture. There is no need for multiple specially crafted salvations for different times and places. The Scriptures spoke of the need of the people of the eighth century BC, or the first century AD, not because they are people of those centuries, but because they are people! It speaks to people today for the same reason.

However, when we see the dominating consideration in the work of exegesis and interpretation as the diversity of historical and cultural moments, we can forget this truth. A person can suggest that God spoke to the people of each time and place where the various parts of Scripture were penned in a manner that was unique to their setting and no other. In that case, the only relevance that the word has to us is in the attempt to design analogies that apply to our day as well as reflect what was occurring to people widely separated from ourselves. In that case, a sharp distinction is drawn between what the Bible meant to those strange people of past ages and how it applies to the people of our era.

When, furthermore, we forget the solidarity of the human race, then we may create a similar dichotomy in application respecting particular people groups. Because of this factor, we see the production of different editions of the Scriptures designed for different demographic groups. Sometimes these are limited to the study helps that are included, but other times this shapes the specific way in which the original languages are translated and paraphrased. So, we have Bibles for women, Bibles for youth, and Bibles for all kinds of minorities.

We need to call biblical scholarship back to a recognition of the solidarity of the race. All the race fell in Adam's first transgression! All the race was and is enmeshed in the tendrils of sin! Humanity needs a Savior! Jesus Christ was sent as that Savior through the blood of his cross. This is the message that every time, place, culture, and language needs to hear.

The Problem of Historical and Cultural Knowledge

Suppose, for the sake of argument, the diversity of historical and cultural matters concerning the biblical text *are* paramount in its interpretation. According to this supposition, the surroundings of the writer and the original audience dominate both what the text *does* mean and what the text *can* mean. What did the writer and his first audience experience and understand? What *could* we expect them to understand?

The logic of these assumptions leads to an inescapable conclusion. The more we understand history and culture, the closer we come to understanding the text. In that positive manner, it sounds very nice and plausible. Nevertheless, the conclusion has a flip side: the less we know about history and culture, the more unlikely it will be that we can understand the text to any significant degree. This may not shock my reader, but it shocks me.

The conclusion shocks me because of the questions raised by it. How much do we know about the history and culture of the ancient world in general and ancient Israel/Judah in particular? The reader may remain unshocked because of the number of learned tomes written on the subject in the last two-and-a-half centuries. Again, it is the question stated in its negative form that is alarming. How much *don't* we know about the history and culture of the ancient world in general and Israel/Judah in particular?

Of course, there is no answer to the foregoing question. It is a tautology of tautologies to say that we cannot know what we do not know. This is true even in the calculation of the quantity of knowledge. Neither is this an example of pettifogging. When compared to the records of our contemporary world and even of the more recent past, the records that we possess of the ancient world are comparatively scanty. The records that existed contemporaneously with that world may well also be massive by comparison. How many missing pieces of data are possibly lost that might radically change our view of those cultures and eras? The historian's lot in life has always been the discovery of new information that throws his theories into a cocked hat.

What conclusions does our God wish us to draw from these considerations? Does he wish us to conclude that we can know very little of the true interpretation of the Bible because new information concerning the history and culture may arise that might nullify the interpretation that we have made? Does he wish us to mark as closed to us great segments of the Old Testament?

To use an analogy, did the groundlings of Elizabethan times have an exhaustive knowledge of the history of the end of the Roman Republic when they watched *Julius Caesar* enacted before them?[1] Was such knowledge necessary for their enjoyment of the drama? If the knowledge was necessary to their understanding and enjoyment of the play, why did they come to see it?

I do not deny that available knowledge is helpful to us in understanding the setting into which God spoke his revelation. However, if it is seen as the determinative factor as to the meaning of the revelation, then the incompleteness of our knowledge of the historical setting will mean an incomplete or faulty understanding of the Bible.

I have spoken of the incompleteness of historical and cultural knowledge at present. What about the greater ignorance of past generations? How much do we know today concerning the ancient world that was unknown to the Reformers or the Lollards? Do we nullify the doctrinal conclusions that they reached from their study of the Scriptures because their knowledge of past ages was less voluminous than ours?

Some in the liberal camp reach this very conclusion. They are not my intended audience. The assumptions Donald Fairbairn mentioned in chapter 1 are not merely their hermeneutical assumptions, they are the assumptions that reflect their view of Christianity. Nevertheless, can we, who cling to the inspiration and authority of the Bible, afford to come to the same conclusions? Can we afford to adopt the same hermeneutical assumptions for the task of interpretation without its warping our understanding of the Christian faith?

I have discussed the limitations of historical and cultural knowledge based upon a scarcity of historical records from the ancient Near East for a period of nearly three thousand years. Yet, within any given epoch of that period, there existed differences of culture.

If one were to ask, "What is the culture of the twenty-first century in North America?" we would properly reply thus: "About which place and ethnic group are you enquiring?" Yet, scholars and pastors speak glibly of *the* culture of the eighth century BC, for example. How much don't we know about possible differences in culture between the nations and people groups of a particular historical epoch?

The Bible itself suggests different cultural norms between people, and sometimes closely related people, living at the same time. For example,

1. Shakespeare, *Julius Caesar*.

Laban explained to Jacob the cultural obligation among the people of Haran to marry off the eldest daughter before the younger is married. Jacob seemed unacquainted with this practice. The fact that Laban was using this cultural practice to justify his duplicity does not mean that he was lying about the cultural obligation. Also, at the time of Joseph, we are told that shepherds were an abomination to the Egyptians, but the case appears different in nearby Canaan.

Can we confidently assume that records of cultural practices from Israel's neighbors truly reflect the culture found within Israel itself? Can we make our *interpretation* of the message of a text of Scripture contingent upon that alleged similarity so that without it, that text has no *discernible* message and, thus, no *discernible* application to us? What do we say about the situation if the assumed similarity is wrong?

These questions are asked upon the assumption, which many make, that the historical and cultural moment at the time of the writing of the text is the sole most important factor in coming to the meaning of the text. If this is the case, any lack of knowledge of these things will bring a tentativeness to our suggested interpretation, even if it is closely connected with the fundamental teachings of the Christian faith.

Paul speaks of an uncertain sound of the trumpet in another context, but the illustration is also applicable here. If historical and cultural knowledge is necessary for the proper interpretation of the Bible, and if there are gaps in our historical and cultural knowledge, then God's people will receive an uncertain sound based on the size of the gaps. Who then will have the ability to prepare for war? Is that situation the position in which God's word places us?

Christian believers yearn to hear from those who would teach them, "Thus saith the Lord!" Will we, instead, give them uncertainty and confusion? Conversely, will we give them arrogant assertions based upon incomplete knowledge, as if wisdom was born with us *and will die* with us? Either alternative is frightening.

A Substitute for Clericalism

At the time of the Reformation, the Church of Rome taught that the true interpretation of the Bible was consigned by God to the teaching magisterium of the bishops with the bishop of Rome (the pope) at their head. This is one of the reasons that Rome was so violently opposed to the translation of the Scriptures into the common languages of the people. They maintained it would tempt them to interpret the Bible for themselves. Consequently, they believed this would lead to all manner of heretical belief in the laity. Instead, the faithful were to give their implicit faith to the teaching of the church and her bishops. This is known as clericalism.

For some time now Protestantism has looked for a substitute term for clericalism. One could call it scholasticism, but that term is already occupied regarding medieval theology. A late friend of mine referred to it jocularly by the term *scholaria*; however, that has hints of unflattering associations about it. I will call it, coining a word as I do so, *professorialism*.

This Protestant substitute for clericalism places the right of interpreting Scripture not with the church and her bishops, as Rome does, nor does it recognize the right to private interpretation, as did the Reformers; instead, it puts it into the hands of the academic experts. According to this perspective, the church, her pastors, and her members must look to them to discover what the Bible means.

However, more than sixty years ago E J. Young in his book *Thy Word Is Truth* said that we should beware of giving over to the experts the question of what the doctrine of the inspiration of the Bible is. He said, rather, that one should consult the Bible itself on this issue.[2] This is admittedly a different question than the view one has of the unity of Scripture. Nevertheless, if a fallible expert can mislead us on one issue, he can mislead us on another issue.

Young does not mention, regarding inspiration and the experts, the possibility of placing the doctrinal teaching of the Bible in a special category labeled *devotional* or *confession of faith*, thus cutting it off from the manner that we use Scripture in the workaday practice of hermeneutics. Instead, Young suggests that the situation is the opposite. He says the question is what the Bible teaches about itself; whether or not one believes it belongs in the area of faith and confession.[3]

If the expert has removed confessional teaching concerning the Scriptures away from the hermeneutical pursuit, the expert can do whatever he likes with the text and still declare that he holds to confessional orthodoxy. In this way, an expert's confessed belief in the orthodox doctrine of

2. Young, *Thy Word*, 17.
3. Young, *Thy Word*, 17.

Scripture may provide no motivation to acknowledge specific doctrines in any of the texts of Scripture.

John Tyndale opposed the clericalism of his era by translating Scripture into the common tongue so that "he who reads may run" (Hab 2:2). It was his conviction that in giving the plough boy the word of God that he could read for himself, he was allowing the plough boy to be as wise in the knowledge of salvation as the bishop in his palace or the monk in his cell. However, if professorialism replaces clericalism, Tyndale's dream for the plough boy evaporates, for, without an up-to-date knowledge of the linguistic, historical, and cultural data of the ancient world, the English translation is as closed to him as the Hebrew, Greek, and Latin.

Even when doctrines seem to jump out from the page of Scripture, the so-called expert puts up his hand and says, "No, no, the people of that generation were not capable of understanding such a truth." That sounds very erudite, but what does one do if it is a text that the New Testament uses to teach the doctrine to the people of the first century? Whom do we believe, God, speaking through his apostles, or man, speaking through the academic experts? God or man, this was, and still is, the issue that E. J. Young saw in the inspiration debate.[4]

I am not saying that we ought to tear down all seminaries (though this is true of some of them), nor do we argue that the church of Jesus Christ can receive no aid from believing scholarship. Nonetheless, there is a difference between aid and domination! The scholars may aid us; we should not allow them to rule us. The answer to clericalism is not the Quaker-like abolishment of ordained ministry, but a ministry duly called by God and under the direction of the word of God free from the trapping of clerical abuse. Likewise, the answer to professorialism is not the forsaking of an educated ministry, but the ministry promoting God's word in the hands of his people in such a way that "he who reads may run."

Jesus said, "And you shall know the truth and the truth shall make you free." He also said, "Sanctify them in truth, Your word is truth" (John 8:32; 17:17 NASB). Was Jesus focusing his remarks only upon the academic expert? Can the humble believer experience the sanctification that comes from God's word? Can they know the word for themselves? Jesus answers: yes!

4. Young, *Thy Word*, 17.

Digging Deeper

The Relationship Between the Old and New Testaments

"The New Testament is in the Old concealed; the Old Testament is in the New revealed," or "The New Testament is in the Old latent; the Old Testament is in the New patent."[5] Do these famous adages mean that we shape and color our understanding of the Old Testament by our understanding of the New Testament? Conversely, does it mean that we shape and color our understanding of the New Testament by our understanding of the Old Testament? Without a doubt, a relationship is implied, but how is that relationship expressed?

One could put the questions in another manner. Is the New Testament concealed in the Old because it has been imported to it after the fact, or was the New Testament theology there all the time but obscured? Is the Old Testament revealed in the New Testament in the sense that the New Testament displays a fulfillment that the Old pointed to all along, or is the Old Testament revealed in the sense that the New Testament writers apply new meanings to the Old Testament texts of which their Old Testament counterparts were unaware?

If we answer the above questions in one manner, we imply that the relationship between the two Testaments is organic. If we answer the other way, we imply that the relationship is synthetic. By definition, a synthetic relationship is an artificial relationship. A synthetic relationship between the Old and New Testaments is compatible with higher-critical views of the Bible. Should this understanding please those holding to its inspiration and authority?

Some say there is no fundamental problem with a synthetic relationship between the Testaments because the person who is responsible for the synthesis is God himself in the person of the Holy Spirit. They say he inserts into specific texts of the Old Testament meanings beyond what their writers intended.

Different scholars in different manners have suggested this path. In a particular stream of Roman Catholic scholarship, there is an appeal to the *sensus plenior*. This is a meaning intended by God but not necessarily by the original author.[6] By this definition, the New Testament writers could be in harmony with the will of God while moving away from the intention

5. Augustine, *Quaestiones in Heptateuchum* 2.73 (PL 34:623).

6. Kaiser, *Recovering the Bible*, loc. 1737 of 4925.

of their Old Testament counterparts. If this is true, then the contemporary interpreter could also move away from the intended meaning of the New Testament writer and still be in tune with the divine mind.

Peter Enns, who was mentioned in chapter 1, attempts to justify a synthetic relationship between the Testaments by what he calls a second reading of Old Testament passages by the New Testament apostles. It is akin to reading a book a second time and seeing specific meanings that were not apparent at the first reading. The analogy is not precise, for the two readings are done by the same person. Such is not the case regarding Old and New Testament writers. The Old Testament, in that regard, reflects the first reading and the New Testament the second.[7]

Surprisingly, other prominent authors, such as Louis Berkhof and J. Barton Payne, also suggest a dichotomy between the Holy Spirit's intention and the intention of the "secondary authors" of the Old Testament.[8] Indeed, the finite mind of men, even infallibly inspired men, can never comprehend the infinite mind of the Spirit.

Some have justified the difference between the intention of Old Testament writers and the intention of the Spirit revealed by the New Testament apostles. Walter Kaiser calls this winning by a technicality, by using wiggle words such as *fully* and *comprehensively* as a description of the incapacity of knowing the mind of the Spirit, even by the inspired men.[9] This methodology implies the portion of the Spirit's utterance was opaque to the Old Testament writers, which partook of his fullness beyond the measure. Yet where does this trajectory stop? Could it not be argued just as plausibly that the Spirit could intend a fuller meaning that actually contradicts or at least abrogates the meaning intended by the Old Testament writer or writers? Yet, the same finitude of which Old Testament writers partook also characterized the writers of the New Testament. Why were they able to comprehend the mind of the Spirit in prophecy and typology more fully than the Old Testament writers who initially gave them?

Nevertheless, I need to raise a more critical issue. How the apostles and other writers of the New Testament proceed does not appear to justify this synthetic view. They often seem unaware that they are giving, through the Spirit, a novel interpretation of the text.

7. Enns, "Apostolic Hermeneutics," 276–78.

8. Berkhof, *Principles of Interpretation*, 60; Payne, *Encyclopedia of Prophecy*, 5.

9. Kaiser, *Recovering the Bible*, loc. 1492 of 4925.

For example, in Romans chapters 9 through 11 Paul argues the case for gentile inclusion in the promises of the gospel and how that truth affects the promises to Israel. To do this, he quotes several times from the Old Testament. In Rom 10:20, where he introduces one of the Old Testament texts, he says, "And Isaiah is very bold and says, 'I was found by those who did not seek Me, I became manifest to those who did not ask for Me'" (NASB). Indeed, this is bold for Paul in *his* context, but if his interpretation is going beyond the intention of Isaiah, why does Paul say, "Isaiah is very bold"? If gentiles were not in the view of Isaiah, why did it take courage for the prophet to make the statement he did? Moreover, if courage was necessary for Isaiah because of something other than gentile salvation, what prompted Paul to mention the boldness of Isaiah? I am unsatisfied with the suggestion that Paul imputed his boldness to Isaiah as merely an exercise in hyperbole. The words of Paul concerning the boldness of Isaiah are extraneous fluff if the relationship between the Old and New Testament is synthetic.

Another example of this will serve for the present purpose. In Acts 8:25–40, we are given the account of Philip and the Ethiopian eunuch. When Philip meets him, the eunuch is reading from Isa 53, and he asks Philip a specific question: "Please tell me, of whom does the prophet say this? Of himself or of someone else?" (v. 34 NASB). Isaiah's intention in the prophecy interests the Ethiopian, and Philip answers him in the context that he lays down. Philip does not attempt to speak of a *sensus plenior* or second reading beyond authorial intent. Should one believe that Philip operated like a modern politician and answered the question he wanted to answer instead of the question asked? This understanding is highly questionable, for the text indicates that from the eunuch's question, Philip "preached Jesus to him" beginning at the scripture that he read. We must reasonably conclude that Philip understood Isaiah's intention of the prophecy that it set forth the Messiah.

Writing in the 1763 preface of a recently republished book by William McEwen, *The Glory and Fullness of Jesus Christ*, John Patison stresses the danger of a synthetic view of the relationship between the two Testaments. He writes,

> The candid reader, who shall be pleased to read the following essay, is desired to take notice that as the discourse itself is not of the argumentative kind, it is taken for granted, as a preliminary maxim, that the grand doctrines of Christianity concerning the mediation of Christ, and the inestimable blessings of His purchase, were typically

> manifested to the church by a variety of ceremonies, persons, and events under the Old Testament dispensation. It is true, there are some who call this truth into question and yet pretend to be friends of divine revelation, but with what sincerity it is not difficult to perceive. For to suppose that the gospel is a new invention and hatched in the age of the apostles, or that the religion of Jews and Christians are entirely different, is signally injurious to them both.[10]

What Is Meant by Progressive Revelation?

Almost everyone who believes the Bible would acknowledge that the revelation God has given to his people is progressive. The very fact that it took place during at least fifteen hundred years and gives a record of events stretching back to the creation of the universe makes this virtually certain. If we speak only of the revelation of the historical record, then we must see progress because history itself is progressive. Yet, progressive revelation does not stop with the progress of history. It also includes those matters that are both doctrinal and ethical. For example, God's curse upon the serpent initiates the promise that finds its fulfillment in the revelation of Jesus Christ as Savior, Lord, and the coming Judge of the living and the dead. Nevertheless, Gen 3:15 does not tell us everything about the Christ of God.

In Romans chapter 5, the apostle Paul, as he builds his argument in comparing Adam and Christ, witnesses to the progressive character of God's revelation. He writes,

> Therefore, just as through one man sin entered into the world, and death through sin, and so death spread to all men, because all sinned—for until the Law sin was in the world, but sin is not imputed when there is no law. Nevertheless, death reigned from Adam until Moses, even over those who had not sinned in the likeness of the offense of Adam, who is a type of Him who was to come. (Rom 5:12–14 NASB)

From these verses, we see clearly that those living between Adam and Moses did not possess the revelation that Moses had. Of course, since this time precedes the written revelation of the Scriptures, we cannot speak of the Bible during this period. Nevertheless, we know that the patriarchs (and others, e.g., Job) were recipients of verbal communication from the

10. McEwen, *Glory and Fullness*, xxi.

Lord, theophanies, and miraculous occurrences, all of which were forms of revelation.

Therefore, we do not question the existence of Scripture's progressive revelation of God's will and purpose. The question is, instead, why is revelation progressive? Many who place exegetical priority on the diversity of the Bible and the humanity of its writers suggest that the reason for such progression is the incapacity of the recipients of revelation at an early epoch to comprehend the revelation given much later in the history of redemption.

Upon what foundation does this suggestion rest? I believe that partially, at least, it rests upon the evolutionary view of the history of religions produced by the higher critics of the late nineteenth and early twentieth centuries to explain the origin and development of ancient religions. According to this view, religion progressed in incremental stages from the belief in a world full of spirits, such as in modern animism. From this, religious ideas progressed to a belief in personal deities associated with nature and natural processes—in other words, polytheism. From polytheism, the ancient world supposedly progressed to a national (or regional) monotheism, which is the worship of one particular god by a people group or nation without the denial of the existence of other gods. From this position, religion progressed to developing a true monotheism that rejected all gods but one. Then came *ethical monotheism* as the last stage in the pre-Christian era that tied morality and religion together. The Trinitarian belief of the Christian church would then appear as a further and unique development. The higher critics saw this progression as the general development of all ancient religions and regarded the religion of Israel as one among the others.

On this basis, scholars divide the Old Testament into the different stages of that development. According to the critics, the religion of Israel began with a rather crude form of polytheism and progressed by stages to a high ethical monotheism.

Suppose one accepts this idea of the historical evolution of Israel's religion. In that case, it is obvious why he would not expect to find advanced theological and ethical teaching in the Scriptures that arose in the early part of the nation's spiritual development. Nevertheless, would this satisfy scholars who reject the evolutionary approach to Israel's religion?

I do not suggest that it does satisfy conservative and orthodox scholars. Yet, when they say that certain doctrines concerning God and his plan of salvation were beyond the understanding of men and women of a particular epoch, upon what foundation do they base that assessment? These scholars ought to check themselves to determine if they have unconsciously adopted certain assumptions from the evolutionary view.

Believing that a doctrine was not revealed at a particular epoch in history is not the same as knowing why this was the case. For example, Gen 3:15, which is all the gospel content that Adam and Eve had revealed to them, does not say that the "seed of the woman" would be virgin-born. Indeed, the naming of Cain appears to make it quite certain that Adam and Eve did not think so. Nevertheless, it goes beyond the text to say that they could not have comprehended such a doctrine. It is far different from saying, on one hand, that they did not know this doctrine because they had no present need for such a revelation, or to say, on the other hand, it was not revealed to them because they had no means of understanding it. The former supposition is as equally tenable as the latter.

One of the myths of modernity is the assumption that contemporary human beings are by nature more intelligent, wiser, and superior to those who lived in the past. This erroneous assumption played a large part in the paternalism that has marked the so-called civilized man's encounter with people groups that were labeled backward and primitive. This, of course, confuses wisdom with technology.

No matter the era one lives in, there are always obstacles to accepting God's revealed truth. The Christian faith is, after all, a *faith*. There is also no obvious reason why it is easier to believe and understand biblical teaching the more advanced one's historical context. It is not the mere passage of time that makes God's truth easier to accept or comprehend. It is growth in spiritual maturity, and this type of growth is possible for believers of every generation.

God the Holy Spirit gives or withholds his revelation according to the disposition of his sovereign will. He also gives or withholds the illumination that makes it possible to understand that revelation according to his sovereign will. Therefore, the idea that later generations are better equipped to comprehend the deep things of the Spirit is a lamentable fallacy. The fact that Nazi death camps are within the living memory of some is witness to the fallacy of believing that the race naturally matures in wisdom or godliness.

Another matter of importance regarding progressive revelation bears repeating. To rightly call revelation progressive, the revelation must progress, no matter how slowly the progression of the truth revealed in God's word was. Nonetheless, there must have been new revelation given at some points. This means that the human capacity of God's people must have been stretched beyond previous boundaries. If not, then the gospel message until the time of Christ would have consisted of no more than the revelation of Gen 3:15. If the horizon of what one understands now is the furthest he will ever know, then that person has come to the end of his existence.

You cannot answer the question of the possibility of the revelation of a certain doctrine by simply asking if it was a new doctrine to the people of the time. If we figuratively place the Old Testament Israelites in prison, the four walls of which are bounded by the knowledge of their fathers and their natural experiences, the revelation of any new truth of the Lord of the covenant has no way of reaching them.

For example, when David said in Ps 110, "The LORD said to my Lord, 'Sit at my right hand until I make your enemies a footstool for your feet,'" (v. 1 NASB) was the concept that the Messiah, the son of David, was also the Lord of David, something that was well known to him already? Or was it something new that stretched his understanding so that he might grow in knowledge, grace, and godliness? Suggesting, contrary to either, that for David the statement had nothing to do with the Messiah is only viable if we to are deny our Savior's statement that David, in the psalm, called the Messiah *Lord* (Matt 22:43).

Let me illustrate another problem with a view that makes the capacity of the reader/hearer the measure of the rate of progression in revelation. Before the fall, was there any incapacity in our first parents of comprehending God's revelation as triune and multipersonal? If so, if they were created "in knowledge [and] righteousness," what was the nature of the incapacity?[11] God did not necessarily need to reveal all aspects of his character to them. There is nothing to suggest, however, that it was *their incapacity* that prevented him from revealing his triune character at that time.

What Was the "Spiritual Norm" in Israel?

Are we to characterize ancient Israel as a generally faithful or generally unfaithful people? Suppose the ordinary spiritual condition of Israel was faithfulness. In that case, the providential circumstances of history and culture could have played a part in the capacity of the people's understanding of *YHWH's* revelation to them. Conversely, if the normal spiritual condition

11. Westminster Standards, Shorter Catechism, Q/A 10.

in Israel was one of unfaithfulness and stiff-necked rebellion, then we could ascribe incapacity, at least partially, to their willful blindness.

I believe that a candid reading of the Old Testament leads to the conclusion that faithlessness was the ordinary condition in Israel. As we read the historical narratives of the Pentateuch, Judges, Samuel, Kings, and Chronicles, unfaithfulness seems to meet us at every junction. The times of spiritual revival are few, and times of spiritual destitution are many.

What was the cause of the incapacity to understand what *we* call advanced doctrinal revelation, and what was the Almighty's response to the inability? Was it the *natural* spiritual immaturity of those living in premessianic times so that God would *naturally* withhold such revelation? Or was the cause unbelief, so that incapacity of their own making would affect their reception of any revelation they received, advanced or not?

The view of the unfaithfulness of Israel as the norm has New Testament support. Stephen's defense of the charges brought against him is a litany of unfaithfulness from the exodus from Egypt up to the murderous hands laid upon the Righteous One (Acts 7:1–53). Stephen's speech is, moreover, a reiteration of the condemnation of Jesus Christ concerning those who in earlier generations murdered the prophets and in later generations built their tombs (Matt 23:30–32).

Above and beyond this analysis of the spiritual condition of Israel is the New Testament teaching concerning the reason for the lack of discernment concerning the "things of the Spirit" upon the part of all men: Jew, gentile, ancient, and modern. Paul writes, "But a natural man does not accept the things of the Spirit of God, for they are foolishness to him; and he cannot understand them, because they are spiritually appraised" (1 Cor 2:14 NASB).

The apostle does not attribute spiritual blindness to the limitations of historical time frames or cultural relevancy but to the absence of spiritual life. A *natural man*, in this context, is an unregenerate man, and this is also true of the Israel of old. One must concede ancient Israel's lack of regeneration unless he wishes to maintain (as Federal Vision advocates seem to do) that Israel was generally regenerated despite their rebellious track record, or unless he wishes to claim that the doctrine of regeneration does not apply to ancient Israel. This latter view creates more problems than it solves, for it suggests that salvation in the Old Testament was significantly different from salvation in the New Testament. This, of course, furthers the destruction of the unity of Scripture.

Those who see the dominance of historical and cultural relevance for the interpretation of the Bible, especially the Old Testament, seem to believe that God did not reveal to his ancient people teachings that they could not grasp. This would mean we can use the standard of historical and cultural relevance as the determining factor of whether or not a doctrine is possible for a particular era. However, a generally unregenerate people are incapable of grasping any spiritual truth, whatever its historical and cultural relevance. Human incapacity, therefore, *cannot be the judge of* whether a biblical truth was revealed or not.

4

Jesus as Archetype and Exegete

Introduction

As implied in previous chapters, there is some controversy concerning how the New Testament uses the Old Testament. The doctrine of the *analogy of faith*, which teaches that Scripture interprets Scripture, has long insisted that the way the Holy Spirit uses the Old Testament gives us the final and infallible interpretations of those portions of the Old Testament with which the New Testament deals. On the other hand, others place a dichotomy between the intention of the Old Testament writers and those who handle their texts in the New Testament. I have noted some of these methods previously. Whether it be the *sensus plenior* of some Roman Catholic theologians or the idea of a *second reading* of Old Testament texts by the writers of the New Testament, as suggested by Peter Enns, a wedge is driven between the two Testaments.

What kind of exegesis is employed by New Testament writers in using the Old Testament? Peter Enns goes so far as to suggest that the New Testament uses the hermeneutic of Second Temple Judaism to bring to the Old Testament texts a *Christotelic* significance beyond the intention of the Old Testament writers. Indeed, not everyone suggesting a difference in intentions between the Testaments adopts Enns's method. Nevertheless, if the use that the New Testament makes of the Old Testament differs from the purpose of the writers of the Old, then we must question what method the New Testament writers employed in the exegesis of Old Testament passages.

This road is a veritable minefield of dangers for those who proceed based on such an assumption. They possibly would conclude that there is no organic unity between the two Testaments. They also may conclude that agreement appears through the Holy Spirit's alteration of the meaning of the text. This suggestion has a whole catalog of problems associated with it.

On the other hand, they may decide there is no absolute unity and that the appearance of agreement is the product of the audacity of the human writers, making the text serve their goals. This last supposition destroys the Bible's unity and damages incalculably one's belief in biblical inspiration and authority.

In this chapter, I will not be dealing with these perspectives. Instead, I plan to look at the New Testament's use of the Old Testament and examine the exegesis undertaken by Jesus and the apostles. First, let us look at our Lord himself as he used the Old Testament in his ministry.

Jesus and the Old Testament

You must include Jesus Christ in the discussion if you believe that the use of the Old Testament by the New goes beyond the intention of the writers of the Old Testament. This is so because Jesus cites the Old Testament in his teaching in the same manner as do his apostles. Anyone who argues differently must prove that Jesus restrained his use of Old Testament in a manner that others did not. We may almost say that the opposite is true. He proclaimed concerning all the Scriptures, "these are they that testify of me" (John 5:39b KJV).

Before we look specifically at Jesus as an exegete of the Old Testament, we need to investigate his overall relationship to the Old Testament from various perspectives. The reason is that Jesus confronts us with the One who is unique in all of history and has an unparalleled relationship with the Scriptures. However, this uniqueness does not say all that I could say about his relationship with the Old Testament. We must look into how Jesus's relationship with the Old Testament appears in Scripture and ask what the relationship means.

The Son of God as the Archetype of Scripture

John's Gospel introduces the concept of the logos as applied to Jesus Christ. "In the beginning was the Word and the Word was with God and the Word was God. . . . And the Word became flesh and dwelt among us" (John 1:1, 14 NASB). Jesus Christ has a unique position: he is the archetype of the Holy Scriptures, presented to us as the Word of God.

Neoorthodox and other scholars have abused this idea. Since Jesus Christ is the living Word of God, they cast doubt upon the Bible as also being a living word. This thinking assumes that the term *word of God* for the Bible is by human contrivance. These scholars suggest that the perfection in the Living Word cannot be transferred to the written texts of Scripture.

Nevertheless, it is not a mere human contrivance that designates sacred Scripture as the word of God. Jesus himself, in his contest with Satan at the temptation, declares, "Man shall not live on bread alone but on every word that proceeds out of the mouth of God" (Matt 4:4 NASB). Moreover, he replies to Satan's devices, "It is written" (Matt 4:4, 7, 9 NASB). This fact shows that the personification of the Word of God attributes perfection to the written word of God.

It is a sine qua non that the Bible, as a type of the Son of God, is an inspired, inerrant, and infallible type. No other type of Christ in Scripture shares this perfection, and those types are all tainted by sin to some extent. Thus, we have the presence of dual perfection: the perfection of the Bible and the perfection of its great archetype.

Far from minimizing the importance of Scripture, Jesus as the archetype of Scripture lends to it a solemn weight. We also detect the perfection that he claims for himself in the writings that point to him, both in the written content as well as the revelation of God to his people.

Jesus says of himself, "I am the way, the truth, and the life" (John 14:6 NASB), and the Bible partakes of those qualities by showing the way, announcing the truth, and proclaiming the words of life. Jesus exercises the offices of prophet, priest, and king. Scripture has a prophetic function in teaching what man is to believe concerning God and what duty God requires of man. In addition, Scripture has a priestly role in disclosing how the sacrifice of Jesus Christ is the means by which God forgives sin. Scripture also has a kingly role in ruling over us through God's commands that speak to us through it.

What does this have to do with the unity of Scripture? If the Bible is a type of "God the Son as the Word of God," then the unity of Scripture is chiefly related to him. Jesus Christ is one person sent into the world with one purpose to which his entire life and ministry were devoted. That one mission was not always clear to others but was always clear to him. His frequent references to his death and resurrection, which befuddled and alarmed his apostles, are witnesses to this awareness of his controlling purpose. If the word of God is a type of Jesus Christ, then the written word should reflect the unity of his person and purpose.

Jesus Christ as the Antitype of Old Testament Types

When we discuss the typology of the Old Testament that leads to Christ, we must be careful not to engage in flights of fancy. For example, some have suggested that the scarlet thread that Rahab placed in her window on the wall of Jericho was a type of the saving blood of Jesus Christ. Not everything that reminds us of Jesus in the Old Testament is a divinely intended type. The English of the New Testament, as translated by the NASB, uses the word *type* only twice: once in Rom 5:14 regarding Adam as the type of him who was to come, and again in Heb 11:19, suggesting that Isaac's reprieve from death was a type of the resurrection. In the first instance, the original Greek is *tupos*, translated as "pattern, example," or the like.[1] The verse in Hebrews in Greek uses *parabole*, used in the gospels to describe Jesus's parables.[2]

On the other hand, there are those who wish to deny that typology exists in Scripture. The only exception they make is when the text makes it inescapable, as in the two passages mentioned above. This practice, too, is dangerous, for unless one limits the types to Adam and Isaac, there will always be a debate as to what constitutes someone or something as being designated a type. There are people, occurrences, and institutions in the Old Testament with typological significance that are clear without the specific language stating the fact. For example, the *goel* or "kinsman-redeemer"[3] (appearing in the law concerning property and inheritance), interpreters generally recognize as a type of Jesus Christ, the Redeemer of his people.

Another matter that needs some discussion is the distinction between typology and prophecy. Confusion can arise when we treat these concepts as the same. In Matt 2:15, Matthew declares that Joseph's taking the infant Jesus to Egypt was the fulfillment of Hos 11:1: "Out of Egypt I have called my son" (KJV). What are we to make of this statement? Did Hosea

1. Bible Hub, "5179. Tupos."
2. Bible Hub, "3850. Parabole."
3. Bible Hub, "1352. Goel."

prophesy of Jesus going into Egypt as a baby? This suggestion has caused some to doubt Matthew's interpretation of the Old Testament text. They suspect Matthew of abusing the text because it seems to be a historical allusion rather than a predictive prophecy.

Notwithstanding, maybe Hosea was doing something other than prophesying the future. Perhaps he was looking backward to the exodus. Perhaps the fulfillment that Matthew saw was typological. Israel, the typical son, was called out of Egypt as Jesus, the true Son, would be brought out of Egypt by Joseph. Notice that Matthew calls his quotation the words of the prophet (Matt 2:15), which Hosea was, not the words of the prophecy. This view allows us to understand Hosea's language without the necessity of concluding that Matthew was abusing the text.

In distinguishing between typology and prophecy, I do not wish to set them as wholly opposed to one another. I am in general agreement with the words of Patrick Fairbairn:

> A type, as already explained and understood, necessarily possesses something of a prophetic character, and differs in form rather than in nature from what is usually designated prophecy. *The one images or prefigures, while the other foretells*, coming realities. In the one case representative acts or symbols, in the other verbal delineation serves the purpose of indicating beforehand what God was designed to accomplish for His people in the approaching future.[4]

Since the primary purpose of this chapter is to examine how our Lord and his apostles used the Old Testament in their preaching and teaching, we cannot make an exhaustive survey of the typology found in the Old Testament that points to the Messiah and his church. But some look at it should be profitable.

Using the word *type* first in the New Testament, the apostle Paul called Adam a type of Christ. The text reads, "But death reigned from Adam to Moses, even upon the ones who had not sinned in the likeness of Adam's transgression, who was a type of the One who was to come" (Rom 5:14). At first sight, this may seem to present a conundrum, for the verse speaks of Adam in connection to his transgression, and the coming One was he who is "holy, harmless, undefiled, and separate from sinners" (Heb 7:26). How is the disobedient Adam a type of the fully obedient Messiah?

Nevertheless, the problem teaches us an instructive lesson. Types of Christ in the Old Testament are not necessarily types because of their

4. Fairbairn, *Typology of Scripture*, 106; emphasis mine.

personal characteristics. In the following passages, Paul shows that Adam was a type of Jesus Christ in that he was the representative head of those who belonged to him through ordinary descent. Thus, we could draw similarities with Christ's sinless character concerning Adam's first creation. Concerning Luke's designation of Adam as "the son of God," we could call Adam typical of Jesus. Still, Paul mentions neither of these things and instead points us to a function that both Adam and Jesus Christ exercised.

We see the second Adam's glory in this typology of function rather than personal characteristics. The type of Adam and his archetype, Jesus Christ, forces us to consider all human beings' ultimate destinies. Adam brings all his posterity, not redeemed by Christ, unto eternal death, while Jesus brings all he represents into life eternal. Note also that Paul's use of Adam as a type of Jesus Christ binds the very beginning of the biblical record to the New Testament. Therefore, from its very inception, the Bible declares its unity.

There is another application of this lesson that should be plain. We might be tempted to trust our intellect above the inspired biblical writer, especially in this endeavor. However, where the Holy Spirit leads us to understand his word in a particular manner, we should not move in a different direction even though our intellect might point us to a different path, however sanctified. This lesson is appropriate beyond the bounds of typology. It applies to all utilization of hermeneutics as it affects the relationship between the Old Testament and the New. In fact, a wise man once wrote, "The salutary lesson of human ignorance is the last to which human pride submits; but a sound philosophy concurs with the sure word of inspiration in pronouncing man to be a creature of yesterday, who knows comparatively nothing."[5]

Moses spoke of Jesus when he declared that God would raise up among the people of Israel "a prophet . . . like unto me" (Deut 18:15 ASV). Is this typology or mere prophecy? It is undoubtedly predictive prophecy because Moses prophetically utters a future occurrence. Nonetheless, this is also typology because we recognize the likeness of the one who speaks and the one of whom he prophesied. There is still a distinction between the fulfillment of the predictive prophecy and the fulfillment of the typology. God fulfills the sign when the prophet like unto Moses arrives and pursues

5. Thornwell, *Theological and Controversial*, 99.

his course. Yet, this is typology because we recognize the likeness of the one who speaks and the one who is prophesied.[6]

How do we know that Jesus is the archetype of which Moses speaks? Why not one of the other prophets that arose in Israel after the death of Moses? This suggestion is rendered impossible in the incident of the rebellion of Aaron and Miriam against Moses in Num 12:1–8. In this passage, YHWH distinguishes how he deals with Moses compared with lesser prophets:

> Then Miriam and Aaron spoke against Moses because of the Cushite woman whom he had married (for he had married a Cushite woman); and they said, "Has the Lord indeed spoken only through Moses? Has He not spoken through us as well?" And the Lord heard it. (Now the man Moses was very humble, more than any man who was on the face of the earth.) Suddenly the Lord said to Moses and Aaron and Miriam, "You three come out to the tent of meeting." So the three of them came out. Then the Lord came down in a pillar of cloud and stood at the doorway of the tent, and He called Aaron and Miriam. When they had both come forward, He said, "Hear now My words: If there is a prophet among you, I, the Lord, shall make Myself known to him in a vision. I shall speak with him in a dream. Not so, with My servant Moses, he is faithful in all My household; with him I speak mouth to mouth, even openly, and not in dark sayings, and he beholds the form of the Lord. Why then were you not afraid to speak against My servant, against Moses?" (ESV)

How do we know that Jesus is not a lesser prophet than the rest? The clue is in the phrase "he is faithful in all My household" and in how this phrase is used in Heb 3:1–3: "Therefore, holy brethren, partakers of a heavenly calling, consider Jesus, the Apostle and High Priest of our confession; He was faithful to Him who appointed Him, as Moses also was in all His house. For He has been counted worthy of more glory than Moses, by just so much as the builder of the house has more honor than the house" (NASB). As honorable as Moses is as the type (and the writer repeats God's commendation), the archetype, Jesus, is incomparably greater.

6. One might conceivably argue that the language of Moses makes it appear that the One he prophesied is a copy of himself. This way of looking at it would suggest that it is Moses, the archetype, and Jesus, the type. A little thought will tell us that more precise language putting Jesus at the opposite end of the simile would be quite clumsy.

Jesus shows himself as the prophet like unto Moses in his unique relation to his Father and the strictly prophetic, priestly, and kingly offices that he exercised. Moses occupied the same three offices as well. For example, Moses had a priestly function, both before and after the ordination of Aaron and his sons.

Since Moses was, by devout Jews of the first century, considered the preeminent personage of the Old Testament, there should be a demonstration that Christ is the fulfillment of that of which Moses was only the shadow. We might say that the theme of the book of Hebrews is to make this very point. The archetype (Christ) is superior to the type (Moses).

The final Old Testament type with which I will deal is David. By some, he is considered the ideal type of Christ. Yet, how do we know that he is a type of Christ? The answer to this question is not as simple as it might seem.

A shared genealogy shows David as an ancestor of Jesus Christ; however, it does not prove that he was a type. Ahaz, for example, is an ancestor of Jesus, but do we want to announce him as a type? Therefore, the shared genealogy does not by itself prove the typology.

As Peter expressed, God gave David a promise with an oath that one of his sons would sit upon his throne (paraphrase of Acts 2:30). This statement is a promise; does it prove the typology? Was this any more than a promise that David's dynasty would endure perpetually? If not, it is no proof that this son would be the archetype of David.

David as a type is based fundamentally upon the Almighty God's analysis of his character. This assessment is given to Samuel before David appears in the historical record:

> Samuel said to Saul, "You have acted foolishly; you have not kept the commandment of the Lord your God, which He commanded you, for now the Lord would have established your kingdom over Israel forever. But now your kingdom shall not endure. The Lord has sought out for Himself a man after His own heart, and the Lord has appointed him as ruler over His people, because you have not kept what the Lord commanded you." (1 Sam 13:13–14 NASB)

David is the one the Lord God describes in this way: "a man after My own heart." The Bible uses him as the standard by which it judges all later rulers of Old Testament Israel and Judah. God also reveals to Jeremiah the shepherd's character that he will give in the new covenant. The prophecy runs in this way in Jer 3:14–16 (NASB):

> "Return, O faithless sons," declares the Lord; "For I am a master to you, and I will take you one from a city and two from a family, And I will bring you to Zion. Then I will give you shepherds after My own heart, who will feed you on knowledge and understanding. It shall be in those days when you are multiplied and increased in the land," declares the Lord, "they will no longer say, 'The ark of the covenant of the Lord.' And it will not come to mind, nor will they remember it, nor will they miss it, nor will it be made again."

The phrase "after his own heart" in Samuel and "after my own heart" in Jeremiah is from the same Hebrew root and differs only according to the changing grammar of the two passages. God's inner being (heart) he sets up to be the model of the man in the two respective passages. They both point to Jesus, typologically in one case and prophetically in the other. Jesus is "the image of the invisible God" (Col 1:15 NASB). He is "the great Shepherd of the sheep, who through the blood of the eternal covenant . . . equip[s us] in every good thing to do His will" (Heb 13:20–21 NASB). And he is the One "who is in the bosom of the Father" (John 1:18 NASB).

Consider the two times when the Father spoke directly from heaven and said, "This is my beloved Son." (See the accounts of Jesus's baptism in Mark 1:9–11 and transfiguration in Matt 17:1–8.) Though this is the Father speaking of his own heart, it certainly implies the heart-centered relationship between Father and Son. Surely, we cannot help concluding that Jesus Christ is the archetypical model: One who is "after [God's] own heart."

I do not claim to have gone as far as the standard orthodox treatments of this matter. I mention typology solely because its value in our understanding of Scripture and our Savior is based on the genuine organic relationship between the Old and New Testaments. If this relationship is synthetic and imposed from without, any typology disappears. In that case, Paul is flatly wrong in suggesting that Adam is the type of the One who is to come. In that case, one is still looking for *the Prophet*, and David is merely an ancestor, not a type of Jesus Christ. There are significant issues at stake when one operates as if the unity of Scripture is simply a theological dogma without any background in the actual pages of Scripture.

Jesus as an Exegete

No one will be surprised that the New Testament contains quotations and allusions from the Old Testament, and what may be surprising is the number that we find. The index of Old Testament quotations in the Aland et al. third edition of the Greek Testament shows approximately three hundred fifty citations, and its index of allusions and verbal parallels lists over two thousand.[7] Those statistics plainly show that Jesus, the Gospel writers, and the apostles used the Old Testament.

A word of explanation is in order regarding the use of the term *exegetes* regarding them. We do not find from either our Lord or his followers the sort of full-blown exegesis found in academic circles. In that case, the New Testament would need to be many times its present length, and its writers *would* write with a different purpose than they do.

However, in their use of quotations and allusions, we find evidence of how Jesus and his apostles wished these Old Testament passages to be understood. It is my firm conviction that they did not quote nor apply the Old Testament in a manner that they believed out of harmony with the intention of the Old Testament text.[8]

First, let us consider the interpretation that Jesus gives of the Old Testament in those texts that he cites. He appears to make free and less cautious use of them, but because, being one with the Spirit who inspired them, he cannot possibly be mistaken in his understanding. As he spoke of these things, he knew both the Holy Spirit's will and the human writers' intention. I wholly depreciate the notion that Jesus was merely a man of his age as any other rabbi in his teaching ministry.

Given the limited space available and the numerous quotations and allusions, I can scarcely scratch the surface in the investigation. Nevertheless, I have chosen those Old Testament passages in which the New Testament use may appear novel.

Jesus's Use of Scripture in the Temptation (Matthew 4:1–11)

Jesus does not strictly give an interpretation of the texts he cites in this passage, and instead, he applies them as he does battle with the tempter. Nevertheless, a passage recorded early in Matthew's Gospel must tell us

7. Aland et al., *Greek New Testament*, 897–911.

8. If this were a more extended treatise about the New Testament's exegesis of Old Testament texts, a necessary subject to cover would be the source of the citations found. I refer the reader to Young, *Book of Isaiah*, 3:143–61, for a thoughtful discussion of this topic. I note that the inerrancy of Scripture influenced Young's interest in the subject.

something of genuine significance about the esteem the Savior possessed for the Old Testament. In this context, he gives us not only examples but also precepts.

The first temptation Matthew records Jesus facing (after forty days of a complete fast) is that he should prove his messianic identity by transforming stones into bread. What is the evil in the suggestion? First, the suggestion tempts Jesus to question the fact that he is the Christ. Second, it suggests an exercise of the power resident in him for a purpose apart from the reason he possessed it. Finally, and chiefly, it asked him to put physical needs and hardships above the matters that pertained to God and his will.

Jesus, not for the last time, responded, "It is written" (*gegraptai*). He then cited Deut 8:3 in these words: "Not by bread alone shall man live, but by every word proceeding through the mouth of God."

We first note that Jesus believed the phrase "It is written" appeals to the authority of Scripture and settles the question. As we find it in Scripture, this phrase does not necessarily introduce one specific citation from the Old Testament scriptures and no others. Jesus teaches us how to deal with the devil by his example of citing Scripture in matters concerning spiritual life and death, and he shows how he is living by the word that proceeds through the mouth of God.

What did Jesus mean when he answered Satan in this manner? Scripture does not tell us in precise words. Jesus was not instructing the devil but combating him. However, when we compare the Old Testament context of the verse cited, we observe similarities to the context in which our Lord found himself. Moses describes how God humbled his people in the wilderness so they might learn to trust him. He shows how the Lord allowed the Israelites to be hungry and then fed them with manna for the entirety of their wanderings (Deut 29:5–6). This experience, said Moses, was to teach them the very truth that Jesus quotes.

Jesus was also in the wilderness, and fasting for forty days and nights allowed him to become hungry. Would God sustain him, his divine Son, as he did the Israelites? However, the Israelites were given the manna as food, whereas Jesus received no physical food. What do we make of this? Is Jesus quoting out of context?

When we look more closely at the Old Testament, it appears that Moses is out of context. How does the provision of bread from heaven teach that man does not live by bread alone? The answer, as William Hendriksen suggests, is found in the language "every word that proceeds through the mouth of God."[9] The Old Testament text says "everything that proceeds out of the mouth of God" (Deut 8:3 NASB). What comes out of God's mouth? The sacred writings, yes, but also his sovereign decrees. God created manna by the *word of God*, just as the world was created by that same decree, as the book of Hebrews tells us.

Moses confirms this understanding of Israel's situation by mentioning God's miraculous preservation of their clothing and bodies; for example, their feet did not swell. Israel was sustained in the wilderness by the LORD's sovereign decrees, which he executed on their behalf. The same sovereign decrees sustained Jesus in the wilderness, and he refused to transfer his confidence to himself. We must conclude that Jesus was applying the words of Moses in Deuteronomy in a manner that is consistent with the meaning of the text in the Old Testament.

By passing on to Jesus's subsequent citation, I resist the urge to comment on the devil's erroneous citation of Ps 91:11–12. I do this because I am looking at Jesus, not Satan, as the exegete.

The devil had suggested that Jesus cast himself from the pinnacle of the temple to see if God would keep him from harm. Jesus responds in verse 7 by citing the first part of Deut 6:16: "You shall not test or tempt the Lord your God." The full citation in Deuteronomy reads, "You shall not put the LORD your God to a test as you tested Him at Massah" (NASB). In the former quotation, Jesus refers to a lesson God taught Israel through Moses. However, here we have not a lesson but a command. The command includes the people's failure to observe it at Massah when they had complained of thirst and questioned God's ability to provide (Exod 17:1–7).

The devil wished Jesus to test his Father's willingness to keep the promised care and protection. Jesus applies the commandment to himself, and because he infallibly understands the devil's machinations, he has interpreted it correctly as it applies to his situation.

Jesus's following citation from Deuteronomy in the temptation account comes in Matt 4:10. The devil has shown him all the kingdoms of the world and their glory, and he promises to give them all to Jesus if Jesus would worship him. Jesus indignantly dismisses him with the words, "Be gone, Satan; for it is written, 'The Lord your God you shall worship and Him only shall you serve'" (Deut 6:13). In the context of that verse, God warns his people against forgetting him, and that he alone is to be the object of their reverence and worship. The LORD meant the command to forbid

9. Hendriksen, *New Testament Commentary*, 227.

the worship of anyone other than himself; such is precisely the use to which our Lord puts it. Jesus's use of this text is obviously in harmony with the Old Testament citation.

Jesus's Allusion to Micah 7:6

In Matt 10:34–36, Jesus uses language alluding to Mic 7:6 and says, "Do not think that I came to bring peace on the earth; I did not come to bring peace, but a sword. For I came to set a man against his father, and a daughter against her mother, and a daughter-in-law against her mother-in-law; and a man's enemies will be the members of his household" (NASB). In the context of Matthew, Jesus was warning his potential followers that allegiance to him would bring potential controversy, persecution, and possibly death. In support of this, he alludes to Mic 7:6 to describe the character of his ministry. He did not come to gloss over the sins and errors of opponents upon the issues of truth and justice. Instead, he came to bring such differences to light even within the family unit. Among other reasons, this was so that Jesus's followers appear distinct from those who rejected him and the gospel of his peace.

As we turn to Mic 7:6, we read:

> For son treats father contemptuously,
> Daughter rises up against her mother,
> Daughter-in-law against her mother-in-law;
> A man's enemies are the men of his own household. (NASB)

In Micah's day, turmoil and contention are everywhere because of the existing unrighteousness. No one is trustworthy: not the community at large, not those intended to protect the community (the watchman), not neighbors or friends, and not even those of one's own family. Micah warns not those who have caused contention and injustice, but those who search for true righteousness and someone dependable.

Micah 7:6 is not a predictive prophecy but forth telling (not foretelling). Neither does Jesus treat it as a prediction. However, there is no discrepancy between Jesus and the prophet here. Yes, Micah's prophetic words characterize his day, but would he be surprised that his warning would apply equally to the days of the Messiah? Jesus uses this scripture in conformity with Micah's intention.

Jesus's Citation of Isaiah 6:9–10

The disciples of Jesus had come to him after the parable of the sower (Matt 13:3–9) and asked him why he spoke to the crowds in parables. Jesus explains an existing separation between those gifted by an understanding of the "mysteries of the kingdom" and those not so gifted. He says the disciples represent the first group, and the crowd at large represents the second (Matt 13:11–12). Jesus mentions Isa 6:9–10 as part of the discussion of God's dealing with the two groups.

Jesus first makes a crucial point for the understanding of Isaiah's words. He says, "For whoever has, to him more shall be given, and he will have an abundance; but whoever does not have, even what he has shall be taken away from him" (Matt 13:12 NASB).

What is he saying? God's gracious gift of the knowledge of his will and his salvation through his word and Spirit begets more grace and more excellent knowledge. At the same time, the hardened heart generates a more severe hardening, which may be called judicial hardening. The understanding of things that pertain to God does not result from a natural process; they are known or ignored consistently with the way the Spirit wishes or does not wish to operate.

Jesus provides an explanation of his speaking in parables, which is an allusion to the verse, "Therefore, I speak to them in parables; because while seeing they do not see, and while hearing they do not hear, nor do they understand" (Matt 13:13 NASB; see Isa 6:9b). Jesus suggests that his parable teaching has a place in the judicial hardening of the unbelieving portion of his audience. Jesus then indicates that his use of parables fulfills the prophecy of Isa 6:10.

Having set the context, let us look at the citation itself.

> You will keep on hearing, but will not understand;
> You will keep on seeing, but will not perceive;
> For the heart of this people has become dull,
> With their ears, they scarcely hear,
> And they have closed their eyes,
> Otherwise, they would see with their eyes,
> Hear with their ears,
> And understand with their heart and return,
> And I would heal them. (Matt 13:14–15 NASB)

Does Jesus's use of the citation in the New Testament match the intention of the verse written in the Old Testament? The only unbiased answer is that it does. The Lord's description and instruction to his prophet accords with the situation that faced Jesus in his ministry. John describes this situation succinctly in his Gospel: "He came unto His own and his own received Him not" (John 1:11 KJV). The situation was not unique to Isaiah; it characterized virtually all the prophets in their ministries, as well as *the Prophet* that was to come. Isaiah's experience simply shows that the servant is not greater than the master.

Some may ask about Jesus quoting this passage in connection with speaking to the multitude in parables. Although Isaiah's prophecy occasionally uses parables, it is not predominantly characterized by them.

In response to this observation, Jesus does not announce the fulfillment of Isaiah's prophecy related to his speaking in parables. In the spiritual condition of his hearers, he finds the prophet's fulfillment. This correlation is where we find the unity of intention from Isaiah in the Old Testament and Jesus in the New.

Jesus's Citation of Exodus 3:15–16

One of the most interesting citations of Old Testament scripture by Christ Jesus is his reference to Exod 3:15–16 during his controversy with the Sadducees concerning the resurrection of the dead. This citation we find in Matt 22:23–33 and its parallels in Mark and Luke. Because the Sadducees desired to humiliate Jesus in the sight of the Jewish people, they came to him with a trick question. They quote the levirate law from Deut 25:5 and pose a situation whereby a woman dies after marrying seven brothers in succession without bearing any sons. Their question is, whose wife will she be in the resurrection?

The Sadducees believed that the doctrine of the resurrection is contrary to the law in that it brings about the possibility of a situation to which the law would have no answer. This question may have been a pet tactic by which they attempted to stump their adversaries, the Pharisees, who passionately believed in the resurrection.

Jesus answers the question despite the malice that lay behind it. He attributes their rejection of the resurrection to their ignorance of the Scriptures and God's power. Regarding the doctrine of the resurrection, the marriage question is a mere distraction, and Jesus dismisses it with the simple response that, in the consummation, there is no marriage between human beings. He says their state is similar to that of the angels, who do not marry.

The essential concern touches on the very nature of God and his salvation. Jesus directed his opponents to the confrontation of Moses by YHWH speaking out of the burning bush. "But concerning the resurrection of the dead have you not read the word that was spoken to you by God? 'I am the God of Abraham, and the God of Isaac, and the God of Jacob;' He is not the God of the dead but the living" (Matt 22:31–32 NASB).

Jesus implies that God is the source of life, having life in himself. His salvation is based upon his power to give life to all who belong to him. That God does so is based on his calling himself the eternal God, the great I Am. He is the God of the patriarchs, who had been dead for at least four hundred years at the time of the burning bush, and Jesus says God does not consider them dead.

Why, some might ask, does this prove the resurrection and not the mere concept of a disembodied life after death? It proves more than life after death because the disembodied state is incomplete.

Jesus correctly understood God's announcement that he is the God of Abraham, Isaac, and Jacob. A man does not make the statement in the Old Testament, *for* it is God himself who speaks! The unity of the Godhead guarantees that he knew all the implications of this verse.

However, we come to the nub of the issue when we ask if Moses, who wrote this record, understood the meaning of the words he wrote. This inquiry, of course, asks if Moses understood the doctrine of the resurrection.

We cannot pretend to see into the mind and heart of Moses. Nevertheless, we can ask what Jesus appears to expect of Moses. He expected the Sadducees to be able to infer the doctrine of the resurrection from the words of Exodus that he cited. The fact that they did not, Jesus implies, is culpable ignorance. If they had the information necessary to make them responsible for understanding the doctrine of the resurrection from Exodus, what did they know that Moses did not know?

Notice that Jesus did not call their attention to his raising Jairus's daughter. He expects them to conclude from these verses in Exodus that the resurrection is a fact. He does not ask them to consider other Scripture texts but this passage alone. Therefore, the data that Christ gave them to examine was not more extensive than that at Moses's disposal. In addition, Moses had recorded the abortive sacrifice of Isaac by Abraham, who, according to the inspired author of Hebrews, expected to receive his son back by resurrection. The same writer also tells us that Moses was among those who sought a heavenly country, not an earthly one, which implies that Moses's faith was set upon the consummation. Therefore, to claim that Moses was utterly ignorant of the inference that Jesus drew from the text is to make a fiat declaration of which there is not the slightest evidence from God's word to substantiate.

Jesus's Citation of Psalm 110:1 in Matthew 22:44

After the Sadducees attempted to invalidate Jesus's teaching, he confronted the Pharisees, the opposing party to the Sadducees, with their teaching concerning the Christ (Messiah) in Matt 22:44. He references Ps 110, one of the most quoted Old Testament texts in the New Testament, due to its explicit messianic nature. We must ask if it is messianic in origin, or is its messianic character based upon a meaning inserted by the New Testament that did not exist in the Old? What will Jesus's citation of it contribute to our understanding?

The context (as Matthew records it) tells of a gathering of the Pharisees to which Jesus asks a question: "What do you think concerning the Christ, whose son is he?" (Matt 22:41b). To the Pharisees' understanding, this was a no-brainer, and they responded, "The son of David" (v. 42). This response prompts another question from Jesus: "How, then, does David in the Spirit call him Lord?" (v. 43). Jesus buttresses this question with Ps 110:1: "The Lord said to my Lord, 'Sit at my right hand until I put your enemies beneath your feet'" (NASB). This citation leads to the final question by Jesus, which forces a conclusion that the Pharisees do not wish to make. "If David calls him Lord, how is he his son?" (v. 45)

Jesus does not deny his Davidic descent. Nevertheless, he claims that the psalm shows that the Messiah is much more than an ordinary human being, and Jesus says he is the One whom David, the greatest of the kings of Israel, calls Lord.

Jesus has structured his argument so that no other conclusion can be made based on the psalm. The question before the reader is, Is this a fair use of the psalm according to its original intention? Did the psalmist intend the psalm to have this interpretation?

One could answer this question in the negative. Nonetheless, by implication, it accuses Jesus of ignorance or conscious deception, which would dishonor our Lord greatly. This conclusion would suggest that David did not write the psalm but someone else, or that David placed himself in the third person so that we should translate the verse as "The Lord said to my Lord"—that is, "David, the king."

If the psalm is not Davidic, then Jesus's attribution to it would be mistaken. If David spoke of himself in the third person by the name *my Lord*, then Jesus was not mistaken about the authorship of the psalm, but he was misleading as to the psalm's meaning. Either suggestion is or should be anathema to any Bible-believing Christian.

We should note that Jesus's pharisaical adversaries do not deny the messianic character of Ps 110 nor deny its Davidic authorship. Therefore, Jesus does not appear to break any new ground in suggesting that David spoke of Christ. The Pharisees are forced into silence by Jesus's final probing question.

The grammar of the first clause of the psalm is no different in the Old Testament, and YHWH speaks to someone whom the psalmist calls *l'adoni* (my Lord). The Hebrew text invites the same question as the Greek citation that Jesus uses. Was David unaware of the import of his language? One has no warrant to suggest it so. The exegetical conclusion to which Jesus pointed is the same as the psalm in its original context must have pointed. It is a different question to ask if the original audience understood David's assertion any better than the Pharisees of Jesus' day in 29 AD.

Conclusion

When Jesus cited Scripture, he made some interpretations that surprised his hearers and some of us. Nevertheless, he did not mention them in conflict with the original intention of the Scriptures. In the case of Exod 3:14–15, Jesus may have pointed to something that was not the main point in the original context, but the subsidiary conclusion was understood. Jesus, in his use of Old Testament scriptures, did not misuse the text of the Old Testament or its intended meaning; instead, he promoted the unity of the Old and New Testaments.

5

The Apostles (and Other Writers of the New Testament) as Exegetes

Part 1: The Gospels as Represented by Matthew and Acts

Introduction

When I use the term *exegete* in reference either to Jesus or those who are responsible for recording his teaching, I do not intend the study to be a technical analysis of the supposed hermeneutical principles they employed when they handled the Old Testament. In the first place, I do not claim the expertise to accomplish this. In the second place, I do not think such an analysis, which must be based upon deductions, is possible. Sherlock Holmes, author of the mythical article "The Science of Deduction," sets down the cardinal principle of that manner of reasoning as, "When you have eliminated the impossible, whatever remains, however improbable, must be true."[10] With all due respect to the great Sherlock, no one may be positive he has eliminated all other possibilities—only those he has happened to notice.

If I may use an analogy, I am not so much interested in how the hermeneutical train of the New Testament writers got to their station but as to whether they arrived at the same station that the inspirational train of the Old Testament writers intended to reach. If the destinations of the Old

10. Doyle, *Sign of Four*, 36.

and New Testament writers differ, it matters little how the hermeneutical principles of the New Testament writers match our grammatical-historical exegesis. If, on the other hand, the destinations coincide, the detailed analysis of the principles by which they arrived still would not materially alter my thesis.

The reasons for my not trying such an analysis pale in comparison with the realization that Jesus Christ is the incarnate God, whose thoughts are not our thoughts and whose ways are not our ways. Any attempt to make his reasoning conform to the limitation of creaturely thought is futile, to say the least, and possibly impious. Did the One who is at one with the Holy Spirit in knowledge and intention need to cite Old Testament texts with a process of merely human reasoning?[11]

Bearing this in mind, in this and the following chapters we will examine citations of the Old Testament made by Jesus's apostles (and others) in the Gospels, Acts, and Epistles. The intention is to continue to show that there is an organic unity to the Old and New Testaments as we interact with them.

Matthew's Use of the Old Testament as a Representative of the Evangelists

I have chosen Matthew to be representative of the evangelists (those who wrote the four Gospels) for a couple of reasons. His Gospel is the first, therefore, it is in his Gospel that one first meets the evangelist consciously citing Old Testament texts and speaking of their fulfillment. Secondly, several of Matthew's citations have been controversial regarding their fidelity to the intention of the Old Testament writers, and if it can be shown that these difficult passages do not destroy the unity of Scripture, then it is more effective than choosing citations in which there is little controversy.

11. Dennis Johnson, in a fairly recent book *Walking with Jesus Through His Word*, argues that in Jesus's discourse with Cleopas and his colleague on the road to Emmaus and later the same evening to the eleven, he teaches them how to approach the Old Testament scriptures to find him. Does this vacate the argument concerning Jesus as a "special case" in terms of hermeneutical principles? I do not believe that it does. First, the approach that Johnson suggests Jesus uses to teach is not a set of exegetical rules; and second, we must allow a difference between a methodology that the Lord taught his disciples as finite creatures and what the divine mind that he possessed can do. Nor do I intend to suggest that Jesus's intuitive understanding of the Old Testament was contrary to sound rules of exegesis. He simply did not need to employ them!

As we deal with Old Testament texts quoted in Matthew, we must distinguish between those citations that he as the evangelist was making, and those cited by Jesus. We have already looked at some of those in the previous chapter. In Matthew's Gospel, a sizable majority of Old Testament citations are made by the Lord himself.

We need to be wary of giving the impression that the Old Testament citations of Jesus are the result of the evangelists putting words in Jesus's mouth. These pious frauds do not help matters but heap dishonor on the evangelist and the One whose gospel he proclaims.

MATTHEW 1:22–23

Matthew begins early in his Gospel to make use of Old Testament quotations. The first one comes in the first chapter, verse 23. In context, the angel announces to Joseph that the child his espoused wife, Mary, was carrying was conceived by the Holy Spirit and that he was to give the child the name Jesus, "for He will save His people from their sins" (Matt 1:21). Then in verses 22–23 we read, "This all took place in order that the word of the Lord through the prophet might be fulfilled saying, 'Behold, the virgin shall conceive and bear a son, and His name shall be called Immanuel, which being translated is, God with us'" (quoting Isa 7:14).

This quotation has raised controversy among scholars, and it has often been suggested that Matthew's use of the text is far beyond the intention of Isaiah and the Old Testament context from which it is taken. Is this the case?

First, the words certainly fit the context of the alleged fulfillment. The virgin, Mary, did conceive and did bear a son, who was the incarnation of God and thus was "God with us." As to the name Immanuel, the angelic direction in naming the child Jesus is good evidence that the evangelist did not intend the name *Immanuel* to be fulfilled in the sense that that would be his personal name.

The context in Isa 7 was the threat to the kingdom of Judah from Pekah, king of Israel, and Rezin, king of Amram. Isaiah is directed to tell King Ahaz that he has nothing to fear from these two firebrands. YHWH promises to fulfill any sign that Ahaz might request, to which Ahaz turns a deaf and hypocritical ear. Responding to this, Isaiah declares that YHWH will himself give a sign. Then follow the words that Matthew quotes.

Some scholars argue that the original context demands the fulfillment of the prophecy within the eighth century BC. They allege that the imminent threat to the kingdom would make a fulfillment in the far distant future irrelevant. In addition, the Hebrew word apparently employed by Isaiah does not mean *virgin* but *young woman*. Thus, it is said that Matthew's claim to fulfillment of this prophecy in Jesus's birth is hyperbole, at best.

The second objection is more easily handled. The word used in Hebrew is *almah* and though the term *young woman* might be used to translate it, more precisely it means maiden or damsel (i.e., a young unmarried woman that would be assumed to be a virgin). It was not Matthew, but the translators of the Septuagint that first suggested the Greek term *parthenos* (virgin), as fitting Isaiah's prophecy. These translators had no Christian doctrine of virgin birth to defend. They must have believed that virgin was the best translation of the Hebrew term. Added to this is the observation made by William Hendriksen that it is hard to imagine that a young *married* woman conceiving a child could be a great sign since it was an everyday occurrence.[12]

The other objection, concerning the timing of the fulfillment, requires a more nuanced reply. One needs to look at the similarities, not the differences, of the contexts of Isaiah's and Matthew's times. A striking similarity is the reference to the dynasty of David in both Testaments. In Isa 7:2, the report of the conspiracy of the two kings is heard by "the house of David," and again in verse 13, Isaiah's response to Ahaz's refusal to ask for a sign is directed to the "house of David." In a passage where Judah's king is the abominable Ahaz, why the reference to David? It is because the Davidic dynasty, not merely wicked Ahaz, is under threat. The projected war of the two kings was to displace the dynasty of David's house by placing "the son of Tabeel" (v. 6) on Judah's throne as a puppet king.

Matthew records the angel's salutation to Joseph as "Joseph, son of David" (Matt 1:20 NASB). This ties the passage to the genealogy of the Messiah that opens the Gospel. Moreover, the next thing that Matthew moves to is the visit of the Magi who first go to Herod the Great to enquire where the Messiah is to be born. This sets in motion the wicked usurping king in his design to destroy the heir of David's dynasty had the wise men returned to him with the location of the Christ. Since they did not return, Herod intended to destroy him as one among many in his slaughter of the innocents.

12. Hendriksen, *New Testament Commentary*, 136.

Hypothetically, had Herod succeeded in his design, the dynasty of David would have expired in the death of the infant Jesus. Therefore, there is a similarity between Isaiah and Matthew in that wicked leaders unsuccessfully attempted to destroy the house of David.

Moreover, there is a thread of dynastic danger stretching from the days of Ahaz to those of Christ. It was successively threatened by Assyria, Nebuchadnezzar's Babylon, Haman the Persian, Antiochus Epiphanes, even by the Maccabean dynasty that was Levitical and not Davidic, and finally here in Matthew by the usurping Herod resting his claim upon his marriage into the Hasmonean line.

The sign that the Lord gives to Ahaz could not deal with the future threats were it to be fulfilled in those days, for who could tell what additional threats to the dynasty would be covered by a sign fulfilled in the day of Ahaz. It must be a sign whose fulfillment would come coincidentally with the fulfillment of the messianic promise and the coming of the One who would sit upon the throne of his father David forever. This did not happen in the eighth century BC, but in the first century AD with the birth of Jesus.

How much of this did Isaiah understand? Further, how much did he need to understand for there to be a unity between the words he pronounced from God in the days of Ahaz and the words of the evangelist in the First Gospel? From Peter's explanation of the knowledge of the prophets concerning the Christ they predicted, we may safely conclude that Isaiah knew neither the exact time nor circumstances of the fulfillment of his prophecy of the Messiah. Nevertheless, we may safely conclude that in speaking of one who was miraculously conceived and given the name Immanuel, he knew that he was prophesying of the Messiah.

The one rough corner to a unity of the two texts is found in Isa 7:16, which appears to say that the birth of Immanuel will take place shortly before the devastation of Syria and Israel. How does one deal with this objection? William Hendriksen suggests that in Isaiah's prophetic vision it is as if the child has already arrived.[13]

Hendriksen may be right in this suggestion. Nevertheless, there is another possible method to handle the apparent problem. Which alternative do the words mean: 1) that the birth takes place *shortly* before the defeat of the two kings, or 2) that the defeat of the two kings will take place *before* the fulfillment of the sign? It is our preconceived notion that *before* means *shortly before* that causes us to insist that the fulfillment must be right then.

13. Hendriksen, *New Testament Commentary*, 139.

It could mean seven hundred years before, for the virgin-born child, Jesus, not being conceived yet, could not choose between the evil and the good.[14] Therefore, what Isaiah is saying, that God will accomplish his deliverance before the sign that attests to it, comes to pass.

Matthew 2:15

The very next citation from the Old Testament that Matthew makes has also been somewhat controversial. This is in the context of the angelic message given to Joseph that he should take the child and his mother into Egypt to escape the rage of Herod. After this narrative, Matthew declares that this was a fulfillment of Hos 11:1: "Out of Egypt I called my son" (NASB).

Many point out that the context of Hos 11:1 is not that of predictive prophecy. From that, they conclude that Matthew is using the citation in a manner that is completely different from its original use. These scholars are correct in their statement of fact but misleading in the conclusion that they draw from it.

The text in Matthew should *not* be read as a fulfillment of a *predictive* prophecy. Matthew talks about a fulfillment of the words of the Lord through the prophet, but there are two types of fulfillments possible—the fulfillment of a prophetic prediction and the fulfillment of a type. Matthew is simply saying that Israel, presented in the exodus as God's son (to which Hosea refers) is a type of Jesus, God's only begotten Son. Why did Israel go into Egypt? Because of the danger of the covenant people being destroyed by the famine. However, to fulfill the promise made to the patriarch, they had to be called out. Why was Jesus taken into Egypt? Because of the danger of his destruction by Herod, who sought his life. However, to fulfill his mission as Messiah, he must also be brought out of Egypt.

Those who wish to maintain that Matthew takes us to a completely different place than Hosea have to prove that when Hosea says that God calls Israel "My son," the prophet has no thought that this was true typologically in the exodus. Specifically, they must show that Hosea did not know that the redemption of God's people in Egypt foreshadowed the redemption

14. When one grants that verse 14 refers to Messiah, as we know Messiah to be, then the question is raised, was there ever a time when he did not know how to refuse the evil and choose the good (v. 15). Was not our Lord conceived in the same manner that Adam was created, in "knowledge [and] righteousness"? Westminster Standards, Shorter Catechism, Q/A 10.

that is found in the Messiah. Why does Hosea look back at the exodus, if not to draw typological significance to the future redemption? How would a mere historical allusion to the exodus promote the prophet's message, if the exodus must be viewed as unconnected to future redemption?

Matthew 2:18

Matthew's citation of Jer 31:15 is admittedly difficult to harmonize with the Old Testament usage. On the other hand, the citation is almost exactly coincident with the Hebrew text. Matthew's passage concerns Herod's order to slay the children of Bethlehem two years old and under. The text begins at Matt 2:17: "This fulfilled the words through Jeremiah the prophet saying, 'A voice is heard in Ramah, weeping and great mourning, Rachel weeping for her children, and she would not be comforted, because they are not.'"

The difficulty does not begin with Matthew's citation of the verse but with Jeremiah's language, for he is alluding to a historical event recorded in Gen 35:16–20. It is Rachel's death in childbirth. Jeremiah, however, is not reciting the historical event as it transpired but adapting it to the inspired purpose.

This is seen in the significant differences between Jeremiah's allusion and the event in Genesis. In Genesis Rachel's distress is not for her children (except insofar as they will be without a mother) but for herself. Jeremiah speaks of a multitude of children but the focus in Genesis is on the one child that is being born. Jeremiah speaks of Rachel's refusal of comfort because of her children's demise, but Genesis shows that refusal because of her demise.

Nevertheless, one need not be concerned with these discrepancies because Jeremiah does not pretend to be reciting history. Rather he is using a historical allusion as a metaphor of what is taking place contemporaneously. The descendants of Benjamin representing the Southern Kingdom (in Jeremiah's day the only kingdom) and the descendants of Joseph representing the already exiled Northern Kingdom are lamenting God's heavy hand upon them, but this comes amid Jeremiah's prophecy of deliverance and salvation. The verses immediately before verse 15 and the verses immediately after that verse make this clear. The refusal of comfort, therefore, is unsuitable in the light of God's promised deliverance and salvation. In the light of such redemption *Rachel* has no reason to lament.

Is Matthew suggesting that Jeremiah was prophetic because of Herod's murder of the children of Bethlehem? One would hesitate to say so. Does that mean that Matthew has abused the citation? Certainly not! I suggest that the word *fulfill* here indicates the completion of Jeremiah's metaphor. The terrible crime of the murder of the children is set in Matthew's narrative amid the coming of Messiah. His ultimate deliverance of his people is the only basis upon which the temporal deliverances of the Old Testament could exist. To whatever hope Jeremiah looked to justify his words of comfort to Rachel's weeping descendants, it was only possible because of the final hope that would be accomplished by the newly arrived Messiah. Therefore, Rachel's weeping in Matthew, like Jeremiah, is set during the joyful birth of Jesus, who "will save his people from their sins" (Matt 1:21).

Matthew 3:3 (Mark 1:3; Luke 3:4; John 1:23)

I come now to a citation that is not particularly controversial. It is, though, one that is found in all four Gospels and representative of the evangelists' use of citations. In the three Synoptic Gospels it comes as the evangelists' comment, and in the fourth, it appears on the lips of John the Baptist.

Matthew 3 opens with the appearance of John the Baptist "in the desert" (v. 3) and his call for repentance because of the coming kingdom. Matthew adds the comment that this happened in fulfillment of the words of Isaiah's prophecy (40:3): "A voice of one crying in the desert, prepare the way of the Lord, make *his* paths straight" (Matt 3:3).

Edward J. Young, in his commentary of Isaiah, says that in context the voice must be that of a human messenger and not a heavenly creature.[15] Then Young says, "Further than that, however, we cannot identify the voice from this present passage."[16] Does this mean that Matthew was going too far in pointing to the Baptist as the unidentified voice? Young disagreed, for he goes on to say that Isaiah purposely hides the identity of the voice.[17] However, if it is hidden, then there must be a time that this unidentified voice will be revealed with the message from God.

This movement from obscurity to public manifestation fits exactly the context in which John the Baptist appeared. His ministry comes as the sudden announcement of the coming kingdom and the coming One. In reference to "make *his* paths straight," the ways and paths he walks belong to him as Messiah and Lord.

15. Young, *Book of Isaiah*, 3:26.
16. Young, *Book of Isaiah*, 3:26.
17. Young, *Book of Isaiah*, 3:26.

As we consider the harmony of this New Testament citation with its Old Testament original, we need to note the way we find it in John's Gospel. Here it is not a comment of the evangelist but the humble declaration of the Baptist.

In the case of the Fourth Gospel, there are only three possibilities. The first is a pious fraud of words being placed on the forerunner's lips. I have already dismissed pious frauds as an activity of the inspired evangelists. The second possibility is that John the Baptist was mistaken in applying the words to himself. This, however, would lead to the conclusion that John was no prophet at all, yet Jesus acknowledges him as "a prophet, yes I say to you, and more than a prophet" (Matt 11:9). The third alternative is that John was speaking of that which he knew and his citation is correct. If this is true, Matthew and the other Gospel writers are making a citation that, according to John, is ratified by the very voice of which the prophecy speaks.

We do not have to believe that Isaiah knew the exact person (who was yet unborn) who would fulfill his prophecy. This is not necessary any more than in the case of the prophecies concerning the *Servant*. In these cases, the unity of Scripture demands only that Isaiah knew that he was announcing the Messiah and his forerunner.

Old Testament Usage in the Book of Acts

Does the book of Acts also show a harmony between the preaching of the apostles and the Old Testament? It certainly does, but it does more than that. Acts gives us a broad view of the apostolic teaching in the first century. Acts has the advantage over the Epistles in the use of citations by showing the harmony of the apostles with one another. We are dealing with the interpretation of multiple apostles and other inspired witnesses; therefore, we can see the harmony of their views in the Old Testament's witness to the Messiah.

The Citation of Psalms 69:25 and 109:8

The first citation from the Old Testament that is found in the book of Acts comes in the first chapter where Peter declares to the assembled brethren that the death of Judas, the traitor, took place according to the foretelling of the Holy Spirit through David. After an explanatory parenthesis that details the circumstances of Judas's suicide, Peter cites verses from two different psalms: 69:25 and 109:8.

Before we examine the citations directly, some preliminary comments need to be made. Acts records here an event that took place before the coming of the Holy Spirit in power. Consequently, some scholars make erroneous conclusions from two dangerous propositions. The first of these is that Peter did not speak under the inspiration of the Spirit, and the second is that the whole process of filling the vacancy in the apostolic college was a mistake.

If these propositions are correct, then the citations, though interesting, do not speak to the purpose of this chapter. They become simply an infallible record of Peter's fallible understanding of these psalms. This view we should repudiate. Even though this was a pre-Pentecost utterance, Peter was speaking in the office of an apostle and, therefore, was clothed with apostolic authority. If Luke considered this event as mistaken, it is remarkable that he included nothing in the text that made his misgivings clear.

There is one matter that we must face squarely. This is the fact that in Peter's citation of Ps 69:25, the statement is in the singular: "Let *his* homestead be made desolate, and let no one dwell in it" (Acts 1:20 NASB, emphasis mine). This is compared to the plural in the Hebrew text of the psalm: "May *their* camp be desolate; May none dwell in *their* tents" (Ps 69:25 NASB, emphasis mine).

We must not attempt to deal with this phenomenon apart from Peter's coupling the citation with the one from Ps 109:8. Psalm 69 is an imprecation upon the speaker's adversaries and the imprecations, including the one in verse 25, apply to the entire category. Psalm 109 is also an imprecation directed toward many adversaries, but in verse 8, the focus is narrowed to one adversary preeminent among them. The general imprecations of both psalms are certainly applicable to the one preeminent traitor. I suggest that because Peter's focus was on Judas apart from any other adversaries of the Lord, he felt justified in applying the general imprecation of 69:25 to Judas. Was not the desolation of a man's household peculiarly appropriate to Judas who died and was deposed in the manner that Luke records?

Nevertheless, was it the original intent of the psalms to speak of the adversary of Messiah and not the adversary of David? The answer to this is found in an exegesis of these psalms with reference to *the analogy of faith*, the interpretation of Scripture by Scripture. Looking at matters from this viewpoint, one must consider that what Peter in Acts says was the *Holy Spirit's* intention in these psalms.

The word Peter uses in Acts 1:16 is *foretells* (*proeipen*).[18] If we are true to the text of the inspired word in Acts, we must interpret these psalms under the guidance of the Holy Spirit as he inspired Peter. *Foretelling* is the term Peter used. Its unambiguous meaning is the telling of matters at a specific time that will be fulfilled at a future time. Peter is, therefore, saying that the psalmist predicted something that would happen in the future. If Peter took language from the past that had no original connection with the future and applied it to the present, there is no foretelling on the psalmist's part. This would be, to coin a term, *post-telling*. In other words, inserting a meaning in the present for words spoken in the past. Such an understanding does not abuse Peter only, but it also abuses the Holy Spirit who guided Peter's choice of words.

Peter denied reading Judas back into the psalms; instead, he says that the Holy Spirit foretold this event through the psalm. The actual manner that the Holy Spirit did so may be open to discussion. The Holy Spirit may foretell through obviously predictive prophecy, but he may also foretell in the way of typology.

We need to be careful in the way we handle typology. It can be incorrectly handled by reading the archetype back into the circumstances surrounding the type by finding language in the Old Testament that, apart from the intention of the text, may be seen to be apropos to something in the life or person of the archetype. This would be typology imposed upon the text, rather than arising from the text. We must guard against finding types where the Holy Spirit has not placed them. Such a practice has the effect of separating the *meaning* of the text when written from the *application* of the text at a future date. I have criticized this practice previously, when exegetes use it to deny predictive prophecy that the Holy Spirit has placed in the text of the Old Testament.

Such a view of typology employed regarding Peter's citation would suggest that Peter was doing the very thing I suggested that he denied when he said that the Holy Spirit was *foretelling* Judas's miserable end through the mouth of David. The Holy Spirit was not *post-telling* the *new* understanding of the psalms through the apostle Peter.

It is true that for creatures who are bound by time that travels only one way, the meaning of the type can only be known when the archetype

18. Bible Hub, "4277."

appears. The Holy Spirit is eternal and speaks of the future because he knows it as a living reality before him.

The Holy Spirit, as he inspired David, may have made use of the circumstances of wicked adversaries in David's life to point by a shadowy finger to the "son of perdition," (John 17:12 NASB) who went to his own place after betraying Jesus Christ (see Acts 1:25). Moreover, we do not need to suppose that David was entirely ignorant of the Holy Spirit's intention in this matter.

This is not to say that typology *must* be how the Spirit's foretelling is understood. David was a prophet and was very capable of the predictive prophecy—for example, "They divide my garments among them, and for my clothing they cast lots" (Ps 22:16 NASB). However, there is nothing in David's life, as the Scriptures present it, that suggests a type of which Jesus's experience on the cross is the archetype.

Peter's Citation of Joel 2:28–32[19]

The speaker is again Peter in Acts 2:16–21, but the circumstances in which he spoke had changed radically. The Holy Spirit in his fullness had descended upon those gathered in the upper room. He gave them utterances in foreign languages, declaring the mighty deeds of God. Jews and proselytes from many parts of the diaspora were present for the celebration of Pentecost. The foreigners recognized the languages as being their mother tongues, but the native-born Jews did not recognize these as intelligible languages and, thinking they were drunk, mocked the believers.

These facts give us an understanding, not only of the circumstance that led to Peter's citation of Joel, but the power and authority by which he cited the passage. It was the power and authority of Christ, through the Holy Spirit. Peter spoke to defend his fellow believers from the mocking charge of drunkenness. Peter repudiated this charge and supplied the proper explanation of the phenomena. It was, said he, the fulfillment of an Old Testament prophecy. Indeed, Peter did not use the actual word *fulfill*, but his language is clear: "But this is what was spoken through the prophet Joel" (v. 16). Peter was saying that the Spirit's outpouring that resulted in the glossolalia was exactly what Joel spoke of in his prophecy, quoting Joel 2:28–32. In Acts, the citation is found to match that of the Septuagint, but it is questionable whether the address was given in Greek. Nevertheless, any

19. Because of its length, I do not include the text of the citation as a whole.

difference between the Hebrew text and the Greek would not affect Peter's use of Joel.

It may be noted that Peter took a liberty in the quotation. He inserted the phrase, "in the last days, says God" (Acts 2:17) in place of, "after these things" (Joel 2:28). Was Peter changing the interpretation of Joel by doing this? It would be hard to make that case. The catastrophic events that Joel said would be seen at the time of the Spirit's outpouring could scarcely have any other reference than the *last days*. The prophecy of Joel demands an eschatological fulfillment, and the apostle Peter provided one for it. In fact, the insertion of the *last days* into the text shows that Peter's intent was to keep the eschatological reference of the prophecy, even though it brings up another question, that of *realized eschatology*, as some call it. In other words, Peter was not willing to take the prophecy out of its eschatological framework, even though it might raise questions such as the absence of wondrous signs in the heavens. There were and are answers to these questions, which are beyond the scope of this chapter to pursue. Nevertheless, Peter's insertion showed a desire to be faithful to the Old Testament understanding of the text when he could have simply quoted the words of the original.

However, the foregoing does raise another question that is germane to the thesis of this book. Was Joel aware of the interval between the outpouring of the Holy Spirit and the consummation of the ages? Peter's use of the text implied nothing about Joel's understanding in this regard. Peter did not attempt to ask the question of *prophetic foreshortening*. He was as silent as Joel upon the subject. For exegetes, nonetheless, the question does arise because it is concerned with the flow of biblical history. This, however, is a subject that neither the prophet nor the apostle touched upon. So, sadly, we cannot make a judgment upon the harmony of prophet and apostle on this precise issue.

The Citation of Psalm 2:1–2 in Acts 4:25–26

Uncharacteristically, there is no precise indication of the one who spoke the words of Ps 2:1–2 in Acts. The citation is given in a prayer of thanksgiving offered by the brethren at the release of Peter and John after they had been interrogated and threatened by the Jewish Council. It is possible through the power of the outpoured Spirit that the citation was made in unison. It is also quite possible that one of the other apostles spoke the words during the prayer. Whoever it was, there is no question that Luke's narrative is an inspired record of the citation.

This circumstance leaves us with a question: Why did Luke include this citation in his narrative? He could have made a general reference to the prayer without including both the citation and the following interpretation of it. Luke, as an inspired writer, had no hesitancy in setting before us these words without a warning as to their competence in reflecting the truth. Moreover, the citation could have been omitted and its interpretation left to be a faithful recitation of the historical events that surrounded Christ's passion. These events happened regardless of whether they are considered a fulfillment of Ps 2:1–2. I proceed upon the assumption that inspiration here includes the contents of the interpretation of the psalm.

In their prayer, the brethren cite the first two verses of Ps 2: "Why did the Gentiles rage, and the peoples devise futile things? The kings of the earth took their stand, and the rulers took counsel together against the Lord and against His Christ" (NASB). They say this psalm finds its meaning in the conspiracy between Herod, Pontius Pilate, the gentiles, and the people of Israel to bring about the death of Jesus. This is noted as a background to the opposition Peter and John experienced. It was also an incentive to pray for boldness to proclaim the gospel. It is noteworthy that after this prayer Luke records, "And when they had prayed, the place where they had gathered was shaken, and they were all filled with the Holy Spirit, and began to speak the word of God with boldness" (Acts 4:31 NASB). Are we wrong in supposing that this divine response is not only a positive answer to their request but a divine approval of their citation of the psalm and its interpretation?

Did the Lord approve the interpretation despite an alleged move away from David's original intent? Was the approval instead because it was according to the original intent of the psalmist? Scholarly consensus actually concludes that the former suggestion must be the case. They insist that the original intent of the psalmist was to present an enthronement song lauding the king in hyperbolic language. The messianic *application* of the psalm is thought to be a New Testament phenomenon of which the psalmist was unaware. This view in the hands of evangelical scholars does not deny the intentionality of the Spirit in the application. Nevertheless, it strenuously denies that such an application was known or even anticipated by the writer or his original audience.

I find myself strongly opposed to such an idea on several grounds. First, it does damage to the unity of the two Testaments. This might be dismissed on the basis that it is grounded in a doctrinal assumption—not an exegetical one. From whence, however, do biblical doctrines arise?

My second objection, though, is an exegetical one. It was well stated by Bishop George Horne of the eighteenth century and reflected in the twenty-first-century work of Walter C. Kaiser. Horne describes a view similar to the one I reject as a view of the double sense of prophecy. This view maintains that the first sense of prophecy is the sense that is intended by the prophet, while the second sense is found in a future fulfillment. Between these two senses, the only connection is found in the bare words. Our satisfaction is supposed to be based upon the uniqueness of the documents and their divine author. Horne's response to this was by quoting a certain Lord Bacon:

> But, that we may not mistake or pervert this fine observation of our great philosopher, it may be proper to take notice, that the reason of it holds in such a prophecy only as respect the several successive parts of one system; which being intimately connected together, may be supposed to come within the view and contemplation of the same prophecy; whereas it would be endless, and one sees not on what grounds of reason we are authorized to look out for the accomplishment of prophecy, in any casual unrelated event of general history. The Scripture speaks of prophecy, as respecting Jesus, that is, is being one connected scheme of providence, of which the Jewish dispensation makes a part so that here we are led to expect that *springing and germinant accomplishment*, which is mentioned. But, had the Jewish law been complete in itself, and totally unrelated to the Christian, the general principle—*that a thousand years are with God but as one day*—would no more justify us in extending a Jewish prophecy to Christian events, because perhaps it was entirely fulfilled in them, than it would justify us in extending it to any other single corresponding event whatsoever. It is only when the prophet hath one uniform connected design before him, that we are authorized to use this latitude of interpretation. For then the prophetic spirit naturally runs along several parts of *such* design, and unites the remotest events with the nearest: the style of the prophet, in the meantime, so adapting itself to this double prospect, as to paint the near and subordinate event in terms of that *emphatically* represent the distant and more considerable.[20]

20. Horne, *Commentary on Psalms*, xiv; emphasis in the original.

Horne is saying that there must be a real providential relationship between the events of the time of the original writer and the events *prophesied* in the New Testament to justify calling it truly prophetic. He says also that some knowledge of this future fulfillment must be in the mind of the writer. Otherwise, the "prophecy is no more fulfilled in Jesus than in any other event of history to which the words are apropos."[21]

Applying Lord Bacon's reasoning to the citation of Ps 2 in Acts 4, we can make some comments. If David was unaware of a prophecy of the Messiah in the words of his psalm, there is no justification for *his* use of the overstated language. The Holy Spirit may use them of Christ, but, if David had no knowledge of this fact, then it does not clear him from inexcusable arrogance in using the language of himself. David was not begotten of God, the eternal destiny of all the kings of the earth does not depend on his favor, and God did not promise David ownership of the ends of the earth. We can excuse David if he knew that the language pointed beyond himself to a greater than he (see Ps 110), but we cannot excuse him if he did not know that.

This general principle Horne sets down in the preface to his interpretation of Ps 2, the psalm that is cited in the brethren's prayer in Acts:

> ARGUMENT—David seated upon the throne of Israel, notwithstanding the opposition made against him, and now about to carry his victorious arms amongst the neighboring heathen nations, may be supposed to have penned this, as a kind of inauguration Psalm. But that "a greater than David is here," appears not only from the strength of the expressions, which are more properly applicable to the Messiah, than to David himself; but also from citations made in the New Testament; . . . and the confession of the Jewish rabbis.[22]

Walter Kaiser says that a prophecy that finds no real connection to the intention of the Old Testament writer has little just claim upon being the product of organic inspiration, since it would deny the Spirit's incorporation of the human intellect and will in the production of such words having "special" prophetic fulfillments.[23]

21. Horne, *Commentary on Psalms*, xiv.

22. Horne, *Commentary on Psalms*, 32.

23. Kaiser, *Recovering the Bible*, locs. 1530–37 of 4925.

Philip, the Ethiopian Eunuch, and Isaiah 53:7–8

The last passage I take from the book of Acts is found in the narrative of the evangelist Philip and the Ethiopian eunuch in Acts 8:26–40. The Old Testament text quoted here is Isa 53:7–8 as cited by Luke in Acts 8:26–27: "He was led as a sheep to the slaughter, and as a lamb before his shearers is silent, so he does not open his mouth. In humiliation *His* judgment was taken away; who will tell of His generation, because His life is removed from the land of the living" (NASB).

Acts tells us that the eunuch was reading this text in his chariot when Philip asked him if he understood it. In response, Philip was invited into the chariot to instruct him. In dealing with this quotation, it is vital that we pay close attention to the wording of the eunuch's question to Philip because the question concerns the *intention* of Isaiah in the writing of the prophecy: "The eunuch answered Philip and said, 'Tell me please, concerning whom does the prophet say this? Is it concerning himself or concerning someone else?'" (Acts 8:34).

Notice that the Ethiopian's question ties the meaning of the text with the intention of the prophet in writing the text. More than this, Philip does nothing to redirect the question from *its* original meaning to its supposed *application*. Philip responded by beginning from that citation and preaching Jesus to the eunuch (see v. 35). Apparently, the text was messianic for Isaiah as well as Philip. Unless we believe that Philip used a faulty exegesis of the prophet to proclaim Christ, we believe that there was harmony between the prophet and the evangelist.

The next two chapters are a continuation of the use of the Old Testament by the New Testament writers in the Epistles of Paul and the General Epistles. Instead of a conclusion, I will close this chapter with an excursus.

Excursus: What's All the Fuss?

Before I examine some of the citations in the Epistles, I am aware of a possible question that may arise in the mind of the reader regarding the extended quotes from Bishop Horne's commentary on the Psalms (see pp. 79 and 80[XREF]). That question may be succinctly stated as, "What's all the fuss?"

Why should it matter to me, or anyone else, whether the citation in Acts was used in the way that David intended? Isn't it the intention of the

Holy Spirit that counts? If the Spirit intended us to apply these verses to a situation surrounding Jesus Christ, then should that not satisfy us? I must confess, it does satisfy many sincere and Bible-believing Christians.

If the whole world were made up of sincere Bible-believing Christians sitting under sound preaching, then there may be no fuss. The facts, however, are otherwise. The world is filled with non-Christians, and it also contains Bible-believing Christians sitting under the teaching of heterodox pastors.

When such persons are confronted with a New Testament that does not tally with the Old Testament, then there is a problem. If even orthodox scholars admit there is a discrepancy between the intentions of the Old Testament prophets and the New Testament apostles, then the unbelievers will begin to draw dangerous conclusions. These conclusions, moreover, may be announced by unbelieving pastors from their pulpits.

Will they not say that the Bible thumpers are playing word games? Will they not also say that the agency of the Holy Spirit as an explanation of the discrepancy is simply an appeal to a deus ex machina?[24] For them, the Holy Spirit is not a living person but a Christian abstraction.

One must take seriously the words of Lord Bacon that Bishop Horne quoted. He says if there is no real connection between the Old Testament and Christianity then there is no legitimate way to deny *any* event of casual history, when the words seem to fit that event. From the perspective of unbelief this casual circumstance may be as relevant to the Old Testament text as the use made by New Testament writers.[25]

The writers of the New Testament use their citations of the Old Testament to prove that the matters of which they write are true. However, if this is a reference to words that were intended for a different purpose, then how does the citation prove anything?

Paul states in Gal 4:4, "When the fullness of time had come, God sent forth his Son" (ESV). If the words of the New Testament do not match those of the Old, how do we know that this was "the fullness of time"?

Jesus said to Clopas and his colleague, "O, foolish men and slow of heart to believe in all that the prophets have spoken! Was it not necessary for the Christ to suffer these things and enter into His glory?" (Luke 24:25–26

24. Deus ex machina: an unexpected power or event saving a seemingly hopeless situation, especially as a contrived plot device in a play or novel. *Oxford English Dictionary*, "Deus ex machina."

25. Horne, *Commentary on Psalms*, 32.

NASB). For the sake of unbelievers, dare we suggest that the prophets did not intend their words so to be construed? Was Jesus rebuking these men for understanding or *not* understanding the Old Testament as it *must have been* understood before the descent of the Holy Spirit?

The church desperately needs a hermeneutic that acknowledges the concordance and not the discordance of the two Testaments. She needs a hermeneutic that sees their convergence and not their divergence. If the world sees us merely congratulating the apostles on finding Old Testament language *that just happens* to *appear apropos* to apostolic teaching, they will not be impressed. Instead, they may see it as justification for their rejection of the inspiration and authority of God's word, as well as a justification for their rejection of the One of whom the prophets spoke.

6

The Apostles (and Other Writers of the New Testament) as Exegetes

Part 2: The Epistles of Paul as Represented by Romans

Introduction

There is a change of perspective as we move from the Old Testament citations found in Acts to citations found in the Epistles. In Acts, the historian Luke—under the inspiration of the Holy Spirit—has selected the sermons, addresses, and other teachings found in the Old Testament citations. We meet several human minds in the Acts study: there is the mind of Luke in his selective process, and there are the minds of each speaker who quoted the Old Testament in his sermon, address, or teaching. That is not the case in the Epistles; we meet only one human mind here.

Does this pose any problem for the study? I do not think so. The unifying factor in Acts, and between Acts and the Epistles, is the mind of God—the Holy Spirit. He was the ultimate selector and guide of the apostles and others in their speech and writing.

Romans as Representative of Paul's Epistles

I choose Romans as representative of the Pauline epistles both because it is placed first in our canon and arguably the epistle that sets forth in greatest detail what Paul called *my gospel.* I say this without intending what I say to be an argument for Romans as a theological textbook. Regardless of the apostle's motivation in sending the letter to Rome, its contents are inspired. Paul draws often on the Old Testament to make his case. It shows many examples of the manner in which he interpreted the Old Testament.

Romans 1:17

The first chapter of Romans contains a citation from Hab 2:4b. It comes in the context of Paul's expression of confidence in the gospel: "For I am not ashamed of the gospel, for it is the power of God unto salvation for everyone who believes, the Jew first and also the Greek. For the righteousness of God is revealed in it of faith unto faith, just as it is written, 'But the righteous shall live by faith'" (Rom 1:16–17).

Unlike most citations previously mentioned, Hab 2:4b is not an example of predictive prophecy or typology. Instead, it is an exposition of biblical truth, both in the original context and in Rom 1. This indeed is forth-telling and not foretelling. Paul was citing Old Testament support for his teaching. He was not claiming the fulfillment of any prophetic prediction.

Some commentators have suggested that the noun in the Hebrew text of Habakkuk, *behemunatow*, is better translated as "faithfulness" rather than "faith." We are told that the root, *emunah*, has a sense of firmness or steadfastness which fits the idea of faithfulness much better than faith. Thus, it is implied that by choosing the Greek rendering *pisteos* ("faith"), Paul was going beyond the teaching of Habakkuk, if not turning it upside down.[1]

One could say that Habakkuk was speaking of *sanctification* while Paul was writing of *justification.* Must one follow this line of reasoning? I do not think so, and some observations might be made to lead us away from this conclusion.

First, why did the translators of the Septuagint employ *pisteos*? Were they so ignorant of Hebrew? Could it be that in the third century BC, Jewish scholars were aware of a broader significance of *emunah* that made *pisteos* an acceptable translation?

A second question comes to mind: Why do so many English versions use the word *faith* in their translations? Bibles choosing this translation include the English Standard Version, the New American Standard Bible,

1. Nicoll, "Habakkuk 2."

the American Standard Version, and the King James Version. Indeed, these versions supply *faithfulness* in a footnote, but the word chosen for the text is *faith*.

Third, is the concept of firmness outside the semantic footprint displayed by the word *faith* (Greek *pistis*)?) If we remember the immediate context of the citation in Romans, Paul was speaking of his commitment to the gospel. Is this not covered by the notion of a firm and confident hold upon the gospel message? Moreover, he writes that the gospel message is the revelation of the righteousness of God "from [or *out of*] faith unto faith."

I suggest that firmness and steadfastness are appropriate to describe the *faith* that firmly holds the gospel as much as these terms would be appropriate to describe the *faithfulness* by which the gospel is lived out.

It would be good to consider the context of the Old Testament: "Behold, as for the proud one, his soul is not right within him; but the righteous will live by his faith [note: or *faithfulness*]" (Hab 2:4 NASB, text and note). The verse contrasts the *proud* and the *righteous*. What is the difference if one assumes the meaning in the second part of the verse as faithfulness? The proud is *not right* in his inner man; how is *faithful living* parallel to this inner condition? In other words, why contrast the inner with the outer? On the other hand, if one assumes the word means faith, the contrast becomes much cleaner. A soul that is out of accord with the Lord is one that, for all its pride, is unstable; but a soul that has found faith is the secure soul.

Let us pay close attention to the matter that a soul *not right* brings us. Is it not a matter of justification? This doctrine answers the question, "How may one be right with God?" Paul's answer was *by faith*, and is this not the answer of Habakkuk?

Romans 3:10–18

This part of the epistle has many citations. They are Pss 14:1–3 (53:1–3); 5:9; 140:3; 10:7; Isa 59:7–8; and Ps 36:1. In uninspired writing, if we come upon a string of widely separated Bible verses, the question of the discredited practice of *proof texting* might be raised. Is this what the apostle is doing, and is the inspiration of the Holy Spirit the only means by which we might see him exonerated from blame? If so, then my thesis of a real harmony between the Old and New Testaments fails.

By what method shall I seek to answer the question? A painstaking examination of each cited text might appear to be the required course of action. However, before we commence that process, it is necessary to understand Paul's argument in the broader context of Romans chapter 3.

Paul begins chapter 3 by asking if there is an advantage in being a Jew and having the mark of Judaism: circumcision. His answer is emphatic: "Much in every way" (vs. 2 ESV). He mentions the most important advantage[2] as the Jewish reception of the oracles (*logia*) of God. After this comes the acknowledgment of Jewish failure to believe these oracles. God is not to be charged with this failure. Rather, this vindicates the position of God as judge.

Paul then digresses in his argument. He wrestles with the counterintuitive concept of unbelief, establishing the righteousness of God's judgment upon that unbelief. This truth Paul argues, despite the seeming paradox of human sin promoting the plan and purpose of God while at the same time leaving God free from any accusation of wrongdoing.

In verse 9, he returns to his argument before the digression: "What then, are we better?" (NASB). Better than whom? The answer to this question is, better than unbelieving Jews. Paul asserts this because he says, "For we have already charged that both Jews and Greeks are all under sin" and sets down the Old Testament citations.

At this point, an exegetical question arises. Do all the quotations teach God's universal condemnation of sin? I must answer this question in the negative, and this answer stands whether one looks at the context of Romans or the contexts of the Old Testament from which they are drawn. Nevertheless, the citations found in Rom 3:10–12 teach this condemnation: "There is none righteous, not even one, there is none who understands, there is none who seeks God. They have all turned away, together they have become worthless, there is none who practices good, not so much as one."

How are we to understand the further citations? They are descriptions of the nature of the sin to which all mankind is subject. The deceit of the tongue, the propensity toward violence, and the absence of the fear of God, all of which the citations mention, describe everyone and his spiritual condition. This is a situation that Paul summarizes in verse 23 with the familiar declaration, "For all have sinned and fall short of the glory of God."

It is relatively easy to show that the citations of verses 10 through 12 in their Old Testament context indicate a universal condemnation of mankind as corrupt. Psalm 14:1 begins, "The fool has said in his heart, 'There is

2. "First of all," I believe, means in this place "first in importance," not first in a long list to which he will never return.

no God.' They are corrupt, they have committed abominable deeds; There is no one who does good" (NASB). If we read only so far, we can imagine that the psalmist speaks of a single group of people that may be called *fools* and that no one within that group does any good. Verses 2 and 3 expel that limitation, for they state, "The LORD has looked down from heaven upon the *sons of men* to see if there are any who understand, who seek after God. They have all turned aside, together they have become corrupt; there is no one who does good, not even one" (NASB, emphasis mine).

The following three citations come from psalms that are pleas for deliverance from enemies, and the specific verses cited are descriptions of the characters of these people. Suppose the speaker of these psalms, directly or by typology, is the Messiah beset by his foes. In that case, we see a description that encompasses *all*, in that he was attacked by the representatives of the whole world, both Jew and gentile.

The citation from Isa 59:7–8 comes from a passage in which the prophet addresses those who have rejected the proffered salvation of God and have been separated from him by their sins. By verse 7, the direct address to these persons has changed to a third-person description of their character. This context also is in harmony with the usage of Paul.

The last citation is drawn from Ps 36:1, which states, "Transgression speaks to the ungodly within his heart; there is no fear of God before his eyes" (NASB). The subject of this condemnation is the *ungodly*. *Ungodly* is in the singular, but it must be seen as a representative figure of all who are ungodly and wicked.

Unless evidence from the texts to the contrary can be shown, one must conclude that the psalmist(s) and Isaiah would agree that Ps 14:1–3 is valid and that the wickedness described is true of all *the sons of men* the eyes of the LORD behold.

ROMANS 4:3 (9), 7–8

Martin Luther maintained that the doctrine of justification is the article of faith upon which a church stands or falls. He was saying that this doctrine is the watershed of orthodoxy. Nowhere in Scripture is the doctrine more clearly set forth than in the third chapter of Romans, and in chapter 4, Paul seeks to prove the doctrine and lay it out for believers.

Paul's proof is partially drawn from the Old Testament cited in the verses of Romans found in the section heading above; these citations are

Gen 15:5 and Ps 32:1–2. Therefore, one needs to know how Paul uses his biblical proof. If he abused the Old Testament intention of these texts, can one comfortably draw the correct doctrine of justification from these chapters?

Yet the importance of these considerations does not stop there. Suppose the Christian doctrine of justification through faith does not find a place in the Old Testament. In that case, it follows that the religion of the Old Testament is entirely different from the religion of the New Testament. Such an understanding would remove the unity of the two Testaments. In that case, no New Testament doctrine could be proved by reference to the Old Testament. This conclusion would stand even if language from the Old Testament were wrenched out of context to support the doctrine.

At the end of chapter 3, the apostle says that the doctrine of justification does not destroy the law. Instead, the doctrine establishes the law (Rom 3:31). In the opening of the next chapter, Paul asks, "What then shall we say that Abraham, our forefather, has found according to the flesh?"[3] Paul then sets forth the issues: "For, if Abraham was justified out of works, he has a boast, but not before God" (Rom 4:2). Accordingly, Paul argues that *works righteousness* is impossible before God. Why is this so? Many theological answers could be given. Nonetheless, Paul believed that this argument was settled by what took place in Abraham's dealing with God.

Here in verse 3 the citation is given, "For it is written saying, 'Abraham believed God, and it was counted to him as righteousness.'" The source is from Gen 15:6, and Paul appears to have taken the quotation from the Septuagint. The sense of the Hebrew text is a little different.

Is Paul in his citation faithful to Moses's intent in Genesis? To answer this question, one must examine the context of Gen 15:1–6. God appears to Abram in a vision to reaffirm the promise to Abram of his offspring. This promise is not in general terms; it is particularized in the promise of a specific son that will be born to him. That was the promise that Abram believed. What could Abram do to bring this promise into being? The answer

3. I have chosen the least popular translation, "our forefather has found according to the flesh," instead of "our forefather according to the flesh has found." I do so for several reasons: (1) It fits better with the argument that will follow. (2) It matches better the circumstance of most of the Romans, of whom Abraham was not their ancestor "according to the flesh" but who was their spiritual ancestor (vv. 16–17). (3) The popular reading makes Abraham's search open-ended (i.e., "what did he find in reference to what?"). The translation I have chosen, matching the ASV and KJV, restricts Abraham's search to what could be found by way of salvation by fleshly endeavor. Having said this, the difference does not materially affect the apostle's argument.

is clearly *nothing*. The *doing* the LORD takes upon himself, and all that is required from Abram is faith.

When one also considers that through this promise, God will bring forth his Son (see Gal 4:4), from whom Abram's son will be a type, then Paul's use of this citation is undoubtedly justified. It is not a general and amorphous faith that justified Abram. It is, instead, a pointed and specific faith in a promise. Moreover, that promise is messianic. It points to both the person and the work of Jesus Christ.

However, is Paul correct in using Abraham's faith in Gen 15:6 as bringing life-long justification? Instead, could it be a faith that brought the favor of God for that one encounter? To answer these questions, one might point out that Abraham's faith was not temporary but continued throughout his life. Moreover, the epistle of James cites this same verse regarding Abraham's sacrifice of Isaac many years later. If the faith of Gen 15:6 was appropriate to that encounter only, how is James justified in using that verse? He can do this because the offering of Isaac was a vindicating act of the same faith that brought justification to Abraham many years previously. The act of faith in the latter case was a validation of the earlier justifying faith that was without works.

Returning to Romans, the apostle says in Rom 4:4–5, "But to the one who works his wages are not reckoned according to grace but according to debt, but the one who does not work but believes in the One who justifies the ungodly, his faith is accounted to him for righteousness" (NASB). This brings Paul to the second citation that is from Ps 32:1–2.

How he introduces the quote is worthy of note: "Even as also David speaks of the blessedness of the man whom God accounts righteous apart from works" (Rom 4:6). What is noteworthy is the summary of David's declaration before he quotes it. This summary emphasizes a difficulty that some have noticed.

In context, Paul has been speaking of a positive imputation of righteousness, and he summarizes the psalmist's statement to the same effect. Nevertheless, when one reads the citation, it does not immediately appear that David's focus is on righteousness, but on the forgiveness of sin empowered by God's refusal to account for the sinner's guilt. Some reading Romans may ask, "How does a negative statement prove the truth of a positive? Does Paul's reasoning break down, and does it take Ps 32:1–2 out of the Old Testament context?"

The apostle quotes, "Blessed are the ones whose lawless deeds are forgiven, and the sins of whom are covered; blessed is the man to whom the Lord does not impute sin" (Rom 4:7–8). This very fact of the non-imputation of sin ought to give pause before accusing the apostle of faulty reasoning or improperly using the Old Testament.

Many commentators are content to say that the negative implies the positive. In this way, they exonerate Paul from faulty reasoning. In the context of the unity of Scripture, one must still ask if the apostle has taken the words out of context. My answer is that he has not, but this requires a closer look at Ps 32.

The words of the citation begin the psalm. Therefore, it is the succeeding verses that tell us the context. Verses 3–5 state the speaker's plight when his sin was unacknowledged by him before the Lord and the relief (i.e., forgiveness he found when he confessed that sin).

One might miss a relevant point if he fails to compare verses 3–5 of the psalm with verse 1. David pronounces blessedness upon those whose sins have been *covered*, and in verse 5, he speaks of his confession in contrast to the silence that brought misery to him. David's confession brings his sin into the open. In other words, it is the very opposite of covering sin, yet David uses verses 3–5 as an application of the truth of verses 1 and 2 to his life. Those verses speak of the covering of sin. What does one learn from this? It is not David's act of repentance that brings the *covering* of sin of which verse 1 speaks, but it must be God's act. Forgiveness, therefore, rests with the act of God, not with the act of man.

What allows David's act of confession to lead to God's forgiving the guilt of his sin (v. 5)? One cannot say that confession of sin in repentance *automatically* brings forgiveness. It is God's covering of that sin, but, as Paul points out in the previous chapter, that must take place so that God is both *just* and *justifier* (Rom 3:26). Therefore, the inner logic that stands behind the argument of Ps 32:1–5 is the propitiation of Jesus Christ. His sacrifice, and his alone, makes it possible for David to move from the misery of the concealment of his sin to the blessedness of God's covering of it. In this manner, David is in sync with the apostle's overall teaching on justification.

As one continues reading Ps 32 to verse 6, a potential problem arises for the Christian interpreter. David seems to exhort the audience of the psalm to do as he has done. Consequently, English translations tie the two parts together, and in the Septuagint, the Greek literally translates, "in behalf of this" (*huper tautean*).[4] The problem comes when David exhorts prayers of repentance to be made by "everyone righteous" (Greek *housios*, "holy, righteous, pious"; Hebrew *chased*, "godly").[5] If the prayer is a confession of sin, how is the one who prays described as righteous?

Once again, we face the truth of Paul's overall argument in Romans chapters 3 and 4. God, says Paul in 3:24–25, has displayed the redemption of Jesus Christ as a propitiation (Greek *hilasterion*)[6] in his blood through faith. The word *displayed* takes us to the actual sacrifice of Jesus, but the phrase *through faith* points to the appropriation of that propitiation by the sinner. It is true that the covering of sin has already taken place in the atonement, where the guilt is canceled. Nonetheless, it is also true that the *experience* of that covering of sin awaits the believer's faith. David can exhort the one who is *godly* to confess sin in faithful prayer because the atonement of the coming Messiah already covers their sins. If one objects that a future sacrifice cannot bring propitiation, he should consider that Jesus Christ is called in Scripture *the Lamb that was slain, and that is in connection with his book of life which is from the foundation of the world* (see Rev 13:8).

However, one is still left with a positive statement needing to be proven by the negative (i.e., righteousness gained by faith confirmed by forgiveness granted through faith). One must not demand that Paul argue by using the same language that one uses in systematic theology. However, there are many scriptures where Jesus's sin-bearing is set forth. As a result, one can speak of justification as a *double* transaction—the transfer of our sins to Christ and the transfer of his righteousness to us. This is the interaction of the *passive* and *active obedience* of Christ. Another biblical perspective considers this as a single transaction, whereby we are by faith united to Christ *in his death*. In this perspective, Jesus is not seen as separate from his people in his passion, but they are present with him and receive the pardon that the passion purchased from that union.

Yet, because that union through faith is also a union with Christ *in his life*, it also carries the righteousness that marks the sinless One. The problem with the perspective that treats justification as a double act is that it can appear to teach a heretical hypothetical. This is the idea that it might be possible to be innocent but not righteous. Such an "innocent but not righteous" state is impossible because Christ's *passive obedience* is said to

4. Bible Hub, "5228. Huper."

5. Bible Hub, "3741. Hosios"; "2623. Chasid."

6. Bible Hub, "2435. Hilastérion."

accomplish forgiveness by sin-bearing, but without his *active obedience*, there is no righteousness.

God calls for *active obedience* in thought, word, and action every moment. His law, therefore, places obligations of righteousness upon us so that failures to act upon them are sins of omissions—not innocence minus righteousness. Righteousness is not simply implied by forgiveness as if it were a foreign thing, but it is necessitated by forgiveness since there is no such thing as a neutral state. The guiltless man is, by necessity, a righteous man because the absence of righteousness incurs guilt. The blessed one, the imputation of whose guilt has been removed, is also righteous through the imputation of that righteousness that must take the place of the guilt.

Did David in Ps 32 connect all these dots? If he did not, he sang of an impossible situation for him and for all to whom his song was addressed. If the sacrifice of Christ was unavailable for him, then on what basis did he experience the blessedness of sins forgiven? Therefore, we may conclude that David understood that he received God's pardon by the act of God in the Messiah that he looked to in faith.

Romans 8:36

Before I leave the book of Romans and the apostle Paul, I wish to look at a citation in which the historical context of the Old Testament is unknown. This is Paul's citing of Ps 44:22 in Rom 8:36: "But for Your sake we are being killed all day long; we are regarded as sheep to be slaughtered" (ESV).

The psalm is ascribed to the *sons of Korah*. It opens (vv. 1–3) with a recitation of God's goodness to his covenant people; and in verses 4–8, the psalmist speaks of the commitment of both God and the people. Verses 9–16 sets up a devastating change in circumstances. The Lord ceases to go out with the armies (v. 9) so that they turn back from their enemies (v. 10), and deportation is implied in verses 11–16. Verse 17 to the end of the psalm is a confession of faithfulness. Moreover, this faithfulness is not merely outward conformity with inner rebellion. The psalmist declares that inner rebellion would be discovered (vv. 20–21). It is from this last section that Paul's citation comes.

Many a historical context might be suggested if the psalm stopped at verse 16. Chief among these would be the Babylonian captivity (see Ps 137). Verses 17–26 make this suggestion impossible because of the claim of the nation's faithfulness. Where might one place this psalm in the contours of biblical history? The exile of the Northern Kingdom by the Assyrians was also clearly a result of their unfaithfulness and equally as impossible as the Babylonian captivity.

One could make many suggestions, but none of them would provide valid biblical proof.[7] Some have suggested that the psalmist speaks in the name of the remnant. Still, there are also problems connected with that view (i.e., the psalmist makes no effort to differentiate himself from the whole of the covenant community who are suffering). Given these vagaries, how shall one conscientiously question Paul's faithfulness to the historical context of the psalm when one cannot say for sure what that particular context was? One may be uncomfortable with Bishop Horne's suggestion that verse 22 is a prophecy of the New Testament church. Still, the criticism is blunted by the fact that there is no specific Old Testament historical setting that can be substituted for his suggestion.

I do not necessarily subscribe to Bishop Horne's suggestion, for I believe that typology explains Paul's use of the psalm just as well as predictive prophecy would. Nevertheless, given our ignorance of the specific setting, it would be wise not to rule the bishop's suggestion out of court.

While it is difficult to find an Old Testament setting that ties the nation's suffering with the innocence of the people, the context of the apostle does this exceptionally well. The apostle asks in the previous verses who can separate the Christian from the love of Christ. He also gives (both before and after the citation) lists of the difficulties that threaten such separation.

The lists include natural ills and man-made dangers. Paul understood that a natural reaction to such matters would be to doubt God's love, and to this he applied a remedy. The ills that threaten the believer here are things that terminate in this life. They cannot pass beyond the grave to harm those safe in the Savior's arms.

The question arises: Why does the Christian have to suffer in *this life*? There is no one, Paul has said, that can bring a charge against God's elect people. They are both innocent and righteous through the atonement of Jesus. Why does a sovereign but loving God permit this? These questions are not stated in the text but are implied in the argument.

7. Exemplifying the difficulty in finding the historical setting of the psalm is the fact that, while A. R. Fausset says that the psalm was written "probably in the reign of David" (Jamieson et al., *Commentary*, 432), Keil and Delitzsch suggest an unspecified post-Davidic setting (see Keil and Delitzsch, *Psalms*).

It is here that Paul brings Ps 44:22 to his aid. Attention needs to be given to how the citation begins: "But for Your [God's] sake" (*eneken sou*).[8] Here is one of the keys to the mystery: the persecution that comes upon the believers is for the sake of Jesus Christ, who suffered to the fullest extent for us. The servants share in the master's reproach, and they do it because he is the King who sends them into the world. The Lord *is* going out with his armies but in a manner that unbelief cannot see and, therefore, will not acknowledge. The New Testament army of God is an army of sheep to the slaughter. They go to the slaughter; nonetheless, they are safe in the "love of God, which is in Christ Jesus our Lord" (Rom 8:39 NASB).

If the Old Testament context of the psalm does not justify Paul's use of verse 22, then what, in that context, does "for your sake" mean? Has the psalmist no inkling of a divine and loving purpose behind the Lord's dealing with his people allowing suffering to come upon them despite their faithfulness? Doesn't the phrase "for your sake" exhibit that he had such a notion?

Again, since I still have to deal with the post-Pauline epistles, I will not place a conclusion at the end of this chapter. I will, nevertheless, put another excursus below.

Excursus: What Did Paul Do and What Did He Think?

The citations from the Old Testament that Paul used in Romans were cited during his composition of the epistle. What was the process by which he included the citations?

The view that we have of the harmony of the citations with their Old Testament context would say something about his answer. If, like me, we believe in a fundamental harmony, then we could picture the apostle being guided by the Spirit to those Old Testament passages that he desired Paul to use. This guidance could take place in many ways. The stimulation of the apostle's memory is one possible method. However, it is also possible that the Spirit placed a passage upon Paul's mind that had not been in his conscious memory. Either possibility suggests an image of the apostle being uninterrupted in the flow of his composition.

If there is no natural harmony between Paul and the writers of the Old Testament, the situation would be quite different. If the only connection of the citation to the New Testament is a fortuitous similarity of syntax and

8. Bible Hub, "1752. Heneka"; "4771. Su."

diction, and if words crafted centuries before merely *appear* apropos to the apostle's argument, then how did Paul come to them as he composed the epistle?

Are we to imagine the apostle pouring over the Old Testament manuscripts as he simultaneously dictated the epistle to find words that would *appear* appropriate? Or did Paul memorize various books of the Septuagint precisely so that he could grasp them for his specific use?

Some experts would ask, Why couldn't the Holy Spirit place these verses upon Paul's mind with a meaning that differed from its Old Testament use? Would such a thought honor God? Is one to believe that the Holy One, who said in the days of his earthly ministry, "Let your yes be yes and your no, no" (see Matt 5:37), would say through the Spirit, "no" in the Old Testament and "yes" in the New, thus changing his meaning at will?

If the so-called experts are correct, was Paul aware that his citations were possibly at odds with the intention of the writers, prophets, and psalmists of old? Did he believe, for example, that Gen 15:6 meant—in the mind of the Spirit—that Abraham was justified by faith, but that Moses did not know of that justification as he recorded the narrative? If Paul was aware of any discrepancy, then why did he give no clue to his readers that the Holy Spirit went beyond the way the words were intended in the Old Testament?

Suppose, it is thought, and rightly so, that the exegete should give due consideration to the organic nature of the inspiration of the writers of the Old Testament. In that case, the interpreter must provide the same consideration to the organic nature of Paul's inspiration.

This is the reason I pose the questions above. The apostle was not in a trance when he composed his epistles. He was not blindly led by the Spirit any more than the writers of the Old Testament were.[9] He must have been intentionally thinking when he cited texts from the Old Testament. Is it reasonable to assume that he had no interest in the original context? Were appropriate syntax and diction his only concern? If the interpreter suggests an understanding of Paul's use of the Old Testament that does not consider these questions, then I do not think he has done a complete job in his interpretation.

9. Some experts believe at least some of the Old Testament writers were in a trance. This makes the picture of Balaam, the alien "prophet," normative for the prophets of Israel (and Judah). It also suggests that the prophetic vision that *did* occur continued in the very composition of the book in which the vision is contained. If this is the case, one must deny organic inspiration for much of the Old Testament.

7

The Apostles (and Other Writers of the New Testament) as Exegetes

Part 3: The General Epistles as Represented by Hebrews

Introduction

I have chosen to make Hebrews the representative of the general epistles for at least two reasons. The first is its relative length compared to the others, thus providing a wide variety of Old Testament citations. A second and more important reason is the writer's consistent use of these citations as essential components of his argument. The argument was addressed to Hebrew Christians concerning the danger of returning to a Christ-less Judaism, and for such an argument the Old Testament citations were indispensable.

This last reason has significant ramifications. The writer's Old Testament citations prove the superiority of Jesus Christ and the religion that centers on his person and work. He wishes, thus, to show that the superiority of the Son is rooted in redemptive history, as illustrated by quotations from sacred Scripture. If he has used the citations in a manner inconsistent with the Old Testament intent, how do they prove his point?

This issue is not an unimportant matter because the writer uses very close reasoning.[1] The Old Testament citations play a significant role in the

1. Close reasoning means that every step in the chain of reasoning is essential, and

writer's reasoning. Therefore, showing that the writer's use of the quotations is contrary to the intention of Scripture would vacate his entire argument.

I intend to show that the case is far otherwise. The consistency of the writer's use of Old Testament references with the plan and purpose of the Old Testament is revealed in the texts he uses. The writer builds an unassailable case based squarely upon the proper use of Old Testament citations.

At the same time, we must not assume that the writer reasons as a post-enlightenment scientist. He does not present theories that he takes to the laboratory of Scripture to prove; instead, he demonstrates the truth by the witness of Scripture through the inspiration of the Holy Spirit.

Hebrews 1:5–13[2]

The writer begins his epistle by drawing a contrast between God's revelation in times past and that which has taken place in these last days. He is not contrasting the meaning of the revelation but the vehicles by which that revelation has been given. God spoke in the past by the prophets through various ways of communication, but now the writer says he speaks by his Son. The Son is both the content of this revelation and the means of communication.

After this introduction, the writer discloses the Son. He is:

- God's appointed heir,
- the agent of creation,
- the perfect and exact manifestation of his image,
- the brightness of the Father's glory,
- the One who upholds the universe,
- the One who purged our sins, and
- now sits at the right hand of the Majesty on high.

The writer says all these things have given the Son a position of superiority over the angels and a more excellent name than they. This last point carries the argument of the rest of chapter 1. He argues by citing the seven texts of Scripture. They are intended to show themselves to be Scripture

---

he omits no link; the logic is precise—not sloppy.

2. This passage of Hebrews contains the following Old Testament citations: Pss 2:7; 104:4; 45:6–7; 102:25–27; 110:1; 2 Sam 7:13; Deut 32:43.

passages that speak of the Son and cannot refer to the angels, or they are Old Testament texts that speak of the angels in a manner inferior to the Son.

The writer introduces the first two citations in verse 5 with the words, "For he said to which of the angels"; then comes the quote from Ps 2:7: "You are My Son, today I have begotten you."

The meaning of the citation is evident in the New Testament context. No angel has ever been addressed as the begotten Son of God. True, in Job, the phrase "sons of God" refers to the angels gathered before the Lord in a general manner (Job 1:6), but the writer of Hebrews states this specific declaration of Ps 2 is unique to the divine Son.

The question is whether the citation is consistent with the context of the psalm. Does the psalmist's intention vindicate the writer's contention in his argument? The overwhelming consensus of evangelical scholarship is that the Old Testament context supports Hebrews only in a *secondary* sense. They insist the psalm is, in its original context, an enthronement psalm in which David speaks of himself hyperbolically. Consequently, the psalm says this of Jesus Christ by way of application only.

Does the writer's argument in Hebrews prove true if this is the case? Does Ps 2:7 prove that Jesus is superior to the angels? This statement would be valid only if we can say that the same verse proves that David is superior to the angels. Yet, this same David says in Ps 8 that God has made human beings "a little lower than the angels" (v. 5). Is David claiming in Ps 2 that he is exempt from the truth that he declares in Ps 8?

Nevertheless, the implication from the scholars is that we do not have to worry about such questions because the Holy Spirit, who inspired the writer of Hebrews, can say anything he wants about an Old Testament text, and it is all right. The citation proves the argument because the Spirit says so.

The sovereign freedom of the Holy Spirit *is* a matter of indisputable truth, but this does not mean that when he uses human language, he uses it out of conformity to normal usage. Instead, the method of exegesis that we embrace is based on the supposition that God speaks to us in human language that is understandable and communicates to us. He even warns us through the apostle Paul that there is a danger when the trumpet gives an uncertain sound. If his words mean one thing in the Old Testament and are used to a different end in the New Testament, is the trumpet's sound clear?

Some will say that I am hoisted on my own petard. These persons will argue that a natural understanding of human language requires the interpretation that assigns the primary reference of Ps 2:7 to David. Is this so? How can one prove that the phrase "I have begotten you" (*yeliditka*) means David's enthronement? The standard Hebrew lexicon by Brown, Driver, and Briggs tells us that this is a figurative usage of God's installation of the king,[3] but how do they know that the language is figurative? They have assumed that the interpretation given to the psalm must be correct. Therefore, the meaning must be symbolic!

Nonetheless, *yelad* is never used figuratively (i.e., as speaking of enthronement anywhere else in the Old Testament). Nor is there anything about the verb *begetting* that brings one's mind to the idea of enthronement. What remains in favor of the argument for enthronement is the observation that the previous verse speaks of God's setting his king (*nasakti malki*)[4] on Zion. Therefore, the phrase "I have begotten you" figuratively means the same thing, according to the argument.

If we follow this argument, why did David, in the Spirit, make no use of the Hebrew verb *yashab*[5] so that the psalm would have read, "Behold, I have set my king upon my holy hill of Zion, I will tell of the decree the Lord has said to me, 'You are My son, today I have caused you to dwell there'" (Ps 2:6–7)? I note that the ESV translates verbs from the root *yashab* regarding God's enthronement (e.g., Pss 9:11; 22:3; etc.). Why pick a verb that suggests no image to match the figure?

However, if David was not speaking of himself but the greater Son, the matter changes completely. Why has God enthroned the Lord Jesus Christ, his Son? Because he is the begotten of his Father. The begetting is not the evidence of the enthronement, but the enthronement is the evidence of the begetting. The begetting is a figure for the enthronement, which God already declared; it is why God enthrones him. If the words are primarily *about* David, then we say that he is figuratively the son of God because he is the one that God enthroned. Such language of the Messiah is backward; he is enthroned because he is the Son of God!

We might ask, Why speak of Zion when Christ's enthronement is in heaven? He also had an enthronement in Zion in his triumphal entry, to

3. See Brown et al., *Hebrew and English Lexicon*, s.v. יָלַד, Qal 3, where Ps 2:7 is identified as a figurative reference to God's installation of the king.

4. Bible Hub, "5258. Nacak"; "4428. Melek."

5. Bible Hub, "3427. Yashab."

the cries of "Hosanna to the Son of David; Blessed is He who comes in the name of the Lord, Hosanna in the highest" (Matt 21:9 NASB).

The writer of Hebrews gives his second citation from the Old Testament, still asking the question, "For unto which of the angels did he say at any time . . ." (Heb 1:5a ASV). This citation is taken from either 2 Sam 7:14 or 1 Chr 17:13 (the wording of the two verses is nearly identical). The quotation reads, "I shall be to Him as a Father, and He shall be to Me as a Son" (Heb 1:5b ASV).

The place of this citation in the writer's argument is the same as the previous quotation, and it demonstrates that Jesus Christ is called *Son* by God in a unique manner. Just as God has said to no angel, "You are My Son; today I have begotten you," God has never told an angel that he is his Father in this peculiar sense. Jesus Christ, the writer of Hebrews declares, is the unique Son of God.

Nonetheless, some might ask, how can this be if this last citation (from 2 Samuel or 1 Chronicles) comes from a historical context that speaks of someone other than Christ, namely Solomon? In the Old Testament context, David determined to build a house, meaning a temple, for God. The Lord tells Nathan to announce to David that it is not David who will build his house but a son who will come from David's own body. This is the one, says YHWH, who will establish the temple. Then comes the language that Hebrews quotes.

Solomon did build a temple to God in Jerusalem. Are we to conclude from this context that the writer has used language in a manner that does injustice to the Old Testament intention? Before we jump to such a conclusion, we should consider some observations. The first is that the words quoted by the writer are words that God himself speaks. David will hear the words mediated through the prophet Nathan, but Nathan hears the words spoken directly by the Almighty. The second observation is that in the same passages, the son of David's body is said to be destined to rule forever. Second Samuel 7:13 says, "He shall build a house for My name, and I will establish the throne of his kingdom forever" (NASB). In 1 Chr 17:14, one reads, "But I will settle him in My house and in My kingdom forever, and his throne shall be established forever" (NASB).

Regarding the first observation, I say that the alleged discrepancy in intention is not between the Spirit's inspired writing in Hebrews and the intention of a human prophet as God's revelation passed through his mind and will. Instead, the imagined discrepancy is God's direct communication to the prophet as against the Holy Spirit's direction of the mind, will, and intention of the New Testament writer. It supposedly sets the purpose of God in the Old Testament in conflict with the intention of God in the New Testament. However, to borrow chess terminology, this is a fool's gambit.

Furthermore, beyond the writer's interest in the relationship of Christ as Son to the Father, the New Testament insists that the church is the house of God that Jesus builds. This is a teaching found in various places in the New Testament. However, this chapter has no space to trace the thread of the teaching concerning Christ and the building of God's true temple in the writings of Paul and Peter.

In the Old Testament context, one sees that the Lord announces to Nathan that David's heir is going to build God's house *and* sit on the throne forever. One also sees that God will call him his Son, and he will call God his Father. Both facts are true of the Lord Jesus Christ. He built the temple of God, which is the church, his body (see Eph 2:22). He sat down at the right hand of the Majesty on high (Heb 1:3). The grounds are insufficient for believing that the writer has taken the words out of context. If there is a secondary fulfillment in the text, it is in Solomon.

The subsequent citation (Heb 1:6b) presents, perhaps, the most difficulties of any Old Testament citation in this chapter. The first difficulty is determining from where the quotation comes.

- The United Bible Society (UBS) third edition of the Greek New Testament lists Deut 32:43 from the Septuagint with Ps 97:7 placed in parentheses.[6]
- The New American Standard Bible cites Ps 97:7 with no mention of Deuteronomy in its notes.
- The English Standard Version quotes Deut 32:43 and Ps 97:7 with a notation in parentheses that the Deuteronomy citation is from a Greek version.

The difficulty increases when one understands that the words cited by the writer of Hebrews appear in the Septuagint and not in the Hebrew Masoretic Text (MT). Usually, a discrepancy between the Greek and Hebrew Old Testament has to do with the precise reading of a clause or sentence.

6. Aland et al., *Greek New Testament*.

Still, here the question arises as to the *possible* insertion into Deuteronomy of language not found in the Hebrew original.[7]

There is an additional difficulty. The words that the writer cites do not precisely match the language of either Deuteronomy in the Septuagint or Ps 97 in Hebrew or Greek texts. This fact makes it harder to determine the origin of the citation in the Old Testament, which may partly explain the variety of ways in which the UBS, NASB, and ESV handle the issue.

Normally, a text-critical problem would be far outside the scope of this chapter. Nevertheless, when one's task is to compare the intent of the quotation in the New Testament with the purpose of the words in the Old Testament setting, we must face the text-critical problem. Certain nonnegotiable presuppositions help us to address the matter:

- The Holy Spirit inspired the writer of Hebrews,
- and the same Spirit inspired the words cited from the Old Testament.
- The Holy Spirit's inspiration directed not only the writer's choice of citations but also the argument for which purpose the words were chosen.

These presuppositions do not answer the text's critical problem, but they safeguard one from making false steps in the answer that he suggests. One cannot guarantee that his answers will be 100 percent satisfying, but a solution that casts doubt upon the integrity of Scripture and he who inspired it is not at all satisfying.

The issue may be clarified by setting the writer's citation before us and listing after it the proposed Old Testament sources:

- Hebrews 1:6b (NASB), "And let all the angels of God worship Him."
- Deuteronomy 32:43 (Septuagint), "Let all the sons of God worship Him."
- Deuteronomy 32:43 (MT), the words do not appear in the text.
- Psalm 97:7b (Septuagint), "Worship Him all His angels."
- Psalm 97:7 (MT), "Worship Him all *you* gods."

We see differences between all the possible Old Testament sources of the citation. In the first case, there is a difference between "angels" and

7. I say *possible* insertion because it is within the realm of possibility that the translators of the Septuagint had access to a Hebrew text that predates the Masoretic Text.

"sons of God." The next difference is the absence of the cited words from the text, as the most accepted Hebrew text now stands. As one moves to the third alternative, he finds verbal form differences. The citation is third person subjunctive; the reading of the psalm in the Septuagint is second person imperative. Moreover, whereas the citation reads "the angels," the psalm reads "His angels." The same verbal discrepancy one finds in the fourth alternative, with the addition of the difference between "the angels" and "*you* gods."

Some scholars suggest the Deuteronomy text because of the identity of the language as they see it. Nevertheless, one can see by previous arguments the significant difference between "all the sons of God" and "all the angels of God." One may concede that the reference may be to the same body of beings, but that tells little in favor of Deuteronomy when the question is the precision of the language. However, the Septuagint's rendering of Ps 97:7 shows similarity in using the subjunctive and the imperative. "Let all the angels worship Him" carries much the same weight as "Worship Him all His angels."

I do not profess to have the expertise to settle this doubt beyond all cavil. Nevertheless, in God's providence, the alternative sources are not without similarity in theme.

Deuteronomy 32:43 comes at the very end of The Song of Moses. It comes in a section in which YHWH declares his determination to bring his vengeance upon his enemies. The preceding verse proclaims God's arrows being drunk with the blood of the slain in the exercise of his vengeance upon the enemy's leaders. The text calls the nations and his nation to rejoice together over this execution of judgment. The inclusion of the Septuagint's words could be seen as a call for the heavenly beings to join the rejoicing and worship for the great victory that God has accomplished.

Psalm 97 speaks of the same theme of God's astounding judgment. Verses 1–6 read like this, according to the NASB:

> The Lord reigns, let the earth rejoice;
> Let the many islands be glad.
> Clouds and thick darkness surround Him;
> Righteousness and justice are the foundation of His throne.
> Fire goes before Him
> And burns up His adversaries round about.
> His lightings lit up the world;
> The earth saw and trembled.
> The mountains melted like wax at the presence of the Lord,

At the presence of the Lord of the whole earth.
The heavens declare His righteousness,
And all the peoples have seen His glory.

Notice that the Lord's glory is revealed in figures and images that bring judgment to mind. These are images of devouring fire, spectacular lightning, and melting at the presence of "the Lord over all the earth" (v. 9 NASB). Verse 6 speaks of this glory as it is revealed in heaven and to the peoples of the earth. Verse 7 tells of the shame of idolaters faced with this glory and adds an appeal for the heavenly beings to worship the God who is glorified.

Therefore, we appear to meet the judgment theme in both passages. Scripture calls both people of the earth and heavenly beings to witness and participate in the worship caused by God's glory and incredible power in the vengeance poured upon his enemies.

If this is so, the citation source in Heb 1:6 could be from either passage without causing a significant change in its fitness to the writer's argument. The question remains: Does the writer's use of the words he quotes fit the Old Testament context of either passage?

Added to the *text-critical* issue involving the source of the citation in Heb 1:6, is the syntax's difficulty in the way the writer introduces the quotation. This phrase has been translated in two different manners. Some translate it like this: "And again, when He brings the firstborn into the world, He says . . ." Others translate it in the following manner: "But, when again He brings the firstborn into the world, He says . . ." The first alternative suggests that the writer wished the quotation to build upon the argument that had already begun. The second alternative makes the word *again* (Greek *palin*)[8] help explain the setting in which the Old Testament speaks the words of the citation.

Is this a matter that can be subsumed under the adage, "You pay your money, and you take your choice"? Some commentators would vociferously deny that such is the case, and they maintain that standard Greek syntax demands a reading like the second alternative.

If these commentators are correct, as I believe they are, it adds an interpretive question with which one must deal before we can move to the citation itself. What does the phrase "when he again brings the firstborn into the world" mean? Given this view of syntax, I see two possibilities that take the word *again* seriously. The first alternative would be that the writer

8. Bible Hub, "3825. Palin."

refers to the resurrection of Jesus Christ, as other scriptures name him "the firstborn of the dead" (Col 1:1 NASB). The second alternative would make this a reference to the second coming of our Lord. This understanding is the option to which I lean, though I would not wish to be dogmatic.

The question that is still before us is, Does the writer's use of the citation fit its Old Testament usage? The syntactical choice that I have made allows an affirmative answer. It is easy to see if the second advent of Jesus is in the writer's view. Indeed, the setting of both the Song of Moses and Ps 97 point us to the very Day of the LORD that the New Testament finds in the return of Christ.

Even if the reference is to the resurrection and ascension of Jesus, there remains an aptness. The resurrection is the inauguration of the last days, and the ascension seats him at the right hand of the Father until his enemies are subdued beneath his feet (see Heb 1:13).

Indeed, since both the second advent and the resurrection and ascension of the Lord reveal him as superior to the angels, the writer of Hebrews is certainly justified in using the citation in the way that he does. One must acquit the writer at this point of any charge of misinterpreting or misapplying the Old Testament.

The subsequent citation that we encounter in this chapter is verse 7: "And of the angels He says, 'Who makes His angels winds, and His ministers a flame of fire'" (NASB). The citation is clearly from Ps 104:4. However, the consultation of the various English translations of the psalm brings forward an apparent problem. This occurs because they translate the similar words of the psalm to read the opposite of Heb 1:7. Instead, they read something like the NASB translation: "He makes the winds His messengers, flaming fire His ministers" (Ps 104:4). One sees the difficulty immediately. The writer of Hebrews intends the verse to be a statement about God's treatment of his heavenly hosts. However, according to the NASB, the psalm assigns literary personification to the physical properties of God's creation. The angelic beings do not receive mention. This circumstance would be nearly fatal for one's understanding of the writer's proficiency as an exegete if it were not the case that both the Septuagint and the Masoretic Text support the rendering given by *our* writer. The translators of the NASB were aware of this fact. A note in that translation informs the reader that the literal reading of the text of Heb 1:7 is as the ESV and others present it.

Why have the NASB and many other English translations reversed the order of angels and winds, servants and fire? The correct reading is not a matter of text criticism, and there are no appreciable textual variants in this case. Two explanations seem likely to me. One is that these translators believed that the context of the psalm fitted a reading that made the reverse order of things advisable. The psalm displays God's power in creation and the order of things doing his bidding. The other explanation is that the translators believed that the literal rendering of the words was a method of saying the opposite figuratively in the psalmist's mind. That is, saying, "He makes His messengers winds and His servants a flaming fire" was figuratively God's use of winds as means of communication and his use of fire in his service. There would then be an exchange of figures, the personification of the messengers and servants exchanged for the personification of wind and fire.

The writer of Hebrews seems content to take the rendering of the Septuagint version as sustaining his argument that the Son is superior to the angels. Moreover, I agree that this literal reading does satisfy his thesis. Yet, if one follows the reading suggested by the NASB (and many other English versions), does the argument of the writer of Hebrews hold? One must be cautious before jumping to that conclusion. Even if the psalmist, inspired by the Spirit, speaks of the angels only figuratively, such language would be improper to use figuratively of the Son. Even as a figure, to reduce the One who is "the exact representation of His [God's] nature" (Heb 1:3 NASB) to impersonal forces of nature would be unsuitable.

Does Jesus not compare the Holy Spirit to the wind in John chapter 3, and does not Luke, in Acts chapter 2, liken the Spirit to fire? Does not this epistle say, "Our God is a consuming fire" (Heb 12:29 NASB)? These things are undeniable, but the questions still hold with the literal rendering of the verse. Whether in figures or reality, equating angels with winds and fire, the writer of Hebrews says this places them in a lower state than Jesus Christ.

We would do well to remember one thing regarding this and the previous citations. The writer's interest is not giving a complete interpretation of the Scripture passages from which he takes the quotations. Instead, he shows that alongside the overall meaning of these passages, they show in their separate ways the Son's superiority over the angels. To make it clear, he has no intention of wrenching the words out of context while doing so, but he does not have to do so.

In the following citation—Heb 1:8–9—the writer turns back to Scripture's testimony concerning the Son with the words, "Your throne, O God, is forever and ever; a scepter of uprightness is the scepter of Your kingdom.

You have loved righteousness and hated wickedness; therefore God, Your God, has anointed You with the oil of joy above Your fellows" (NASB). The aptness of the writer's argument is crystal clear. The One in this phrase is addressed as God, but God anoints him because of his righteous rule. Obviously, the recipient of this praise is superior to the angelic host. Yet, is the recipient the Son? Who else could it be without blasphemy?

Nevertheless, C. John Collins suggests that the psalmist here is addressing God concerning the divine throne, upon which the Davidic king sits, and concerning the righteous scepter, which ideally the king is supposed to wield.[9] This interpretation is seriously flawed and escapes blasphemy only by ignoring grammatical constructs. A connection exists between the statement addressed to God, as the owner of the *eternal* throne, and the one speaking of his scepter. This connection ties the impeccable moral character of the One addressed to his anointing beyond his companions. The link is *thus* (*ken*)[10] in the Hebrew of the psalm. How do God's eternal throne, his righteous scepter, and his impeccable moral character become the reason for a human king's anointing? It is probable Collins would say that it is the Old Testament king who displays this impeccable moral nature. Still, there is nothing in the grammar of the Hebrew (or Greek) text that tells us that the *your* of the words concerning the throne and scepter is not the same as the *you* that describes the righteous character of the one who is addressed.

Collins is aware that the writer of Hebrews uses 1:8–9 to support the argument that the Son is superior to the angels. He seems content to suggest that the writer sees Jesus as David's *heir* so that the words the psalm speaks about David's heir would be spoken about Jesus. This understanding will not suffice. The writer of Hebrews introduces the term *Son* as "the heir of all things" (Heb 1:2 NASB) and not merely the heir of David. He is the brightness of God's glory and the exact representation of his image. He is the One who upholds *all things* by the word of his power. The title *Son* represents God's entire revelation of himself in "these last days" (v. 2). To make the title merely a Davidic family name does much harm to the context of Hebrews chapter 1. One needs to ask Collins a question like the one Jesus asked the Pharisees: If he is David's son, how is he David's Creator?

The writer presents all of the chapter 1 citations as matters that God says (*legei*)[11] concerning either his Son or the angels. Therefore, it is not an

9. Collins, *ESV Study Bible*, Ps 45:6–7 (993n3).

10. Bible Hub, "3651. Ken."

11. Bible Hub, "3004. Legó."

issue of how the writer wishes to use them but an issue of the intention of the God who spoke them.

As we come to the citation in Heb 1:10–12 from Ps 102:25–27, it is good to remember something said at the beginning of this chapter. The writer does not argue that his citations were laboratory proofs of a theory he has propounded. Instead, he demonstrates the truth that he has set forth by the witness of the Old Testament.

We would do well to remember the cumulative nature of the Hebrew writer's argument in chapter 1. It is not as though each citation is a hermetically sealed proof so that each succeeding citation is viewed from ground zero, where nothing is assumed to be known. It is upon the basis of what he has already demonstrated that he moves on to the subsequent citation. He has already shown from Ps 2 and 2 Sam 7 that Jesus Christ is called God's Son. He has demonstrated that the angelic beings are commanded to worship him and that by contrast, the angels are beings that God uses to serve him at his will. The writer has already demonstrated that Jesus Christ is the One who sits upon an eternal throne exercising a righteous rule to which the Spirit has anointed him beyond the capacity of any rival. We do not need to demonstrate any of this again. We would do well to look for another truth demonstrated by this citation.

The citation reads thus: "You, Lord, in the beginning laid the foundation of the earth, and the heavens are the works of Your hands; they will perish, but You remain; and they all will become old like a garment, and like a mantle You will roll them up; like a garment they will also be changed. But You are the same, and Your years will not come to an end" (Heb 1:10–12 NASB). The writer introduces the citation by the simple word *and* (*kai* in Greek)[12] that brings us to the introduction of the previous citation: "but concerning the Son *He says*" (Heb 1:8). The italicized insertion takes one further back to verse 6, which also supplies the "He says." These words and phrases tie the present citation to what has gone before.

If one demands clear evidence from Ps 102 that the psalmist speaks specifically of the Son, then the demand is vainly put forward. Such a demand assumes that the writer is attempting to *show again* that the psalmist calls the Son God. However, since the argument is cumulative, the writer cites Ps 102, not to prove that Jesus as the Son is God, but *because* he is God, the citation is true of him. He has demonstrated the Son's divinity through the previous quotations. He now draws upon Ps 102:25–27 to show that the

12. Bible Hub, "2532. Kai."

Old Testament presents the One who is God as the eternal Creator, who is set apart from all else, including the angels.

For those readers who are uncomfortable stating things in such a manner, it is essential to remember that orthodox Christians are not tritheists, as Islam imagines, but Trinitarians. Each of the three persons of the Godhead possesses all that pertains to the divine nature. The distinction of persons in no sense annihilates the unity of God's essence. Deity is not like humanity (i.e., a general description of existence shared by many individual beings). That God is One is not a predication that might be otherwise. Instead, it is the sine qua non of deity. Just as the absolute distinction of the three persons does not erase the unity, the unity does not dissolve the persons into modes of existence. This understanding is how one views the references to deity, whether by this writer or the other New Testament writers.

The last citation that the writer makes in the first chapter is from Ps 110:1. He introduces it in virtually the same manner that he introduced the first citation. He writes, "But to which of the angels has He said at any time, sit at my right hand until I make your enemies *as* a footstool for your feet" (Heb 1:13 NASB, emphasis mine).

This quotation and the following statement of the angels as God's servants concludes the argument he has been making concerning the superiority of Jesus Christ over the angels. The citation also demonstrates the truth of the writer's declaration in verse 3 that the Son is seated "at the right hand of the Majesty on High" (Heb 1:3 NASB).[13]

Even C. John Collins recognizes that the One spoken of as *my Lord* is the Messiah, and thus it is he who sits at God's right hand. Yet Collins suggests this insight is brought to light only by Jesus's commentary on the

13. Nor is this the only citation that does more than barely demonstrate the superiority of the Son over the angels. The previous citations also show the Old Testament witness to other matters the writer has declared. In declaring Jesus Christ to be the Son of God, begotten of the Father (Ps 2), the writer implies that he is the "exact representation of [God's] image" (Heb 1:3 NASB). When the writer infers from Ps 45 that Jesus is the One who sits as God upon an eternal throne, he implies a universal reign. A reign, though it focuses upon a rule over moral agents (the scepter of righteousness), also declares Christ's authority over all creation as the One upholding all things by the word of his power. The writer confirms this thought in the citation of Ps 103, showing that Christ is the One through whom God made the world. At the same time, this demonstrates that he will also bring the first creation to an end. In setting Jesus Christ in control of the beginning creation and the ending consummation, the Scriptures imply that he has authority over everything between the two extremes.

psalm in Matt 22 and synoptic parallels. He points out that the throne of Israel is called "the throne of the Lord" in 1 Chr 29:23.

Indeed, the throne of Israel was God's throne because God was the true King of Israel. Nevertheless, Israel was merely an earthly kingdom that had boundaries. Conversely, the throne at God's right hand is universal, and the One upon which David and Solomon sat was only a type of the throne upon which Jesus Christ sits.

For the argument of the writer of Hebrews to stand, one must acknowledge that sitting at the right hand of God is a place of unique authority that gives the occupant a name that is more excellent than that of the angels. Nevertheless, Jesus, as he uses the psalm, does not suggest he is importing a new insight into the words, for he implies that this was David's intention, speaking in the Spirit. If this is true of the psalm, as it addresses *My Lord*, it is undoubtedly true concerning the content of the address: "Sit at My right hand, until I make Your enemies a footstool for Your feet" (Ps 110:1 NASB).

Hebrews 5:5–6 (Psalms 2:7; 110:4); Hebrews 7:17, 21 (Psalm 110:4)

In Heb 5, the writer couples the citation of Ps 110:4 with a quotation from Ps 2:7. At the end of the fourth chapter, the writer urges his readers to find consolation from the Christian's high priest, Jesus Christ, who can sympathize with us in our weakness. This thought brings him to begin chapter five with a discussion concerning Jesus as the perfect high priest.

The discussion is arrested in chapter 6, where there is a digression concerning the danger of apostasy of those who, having once embraced Christ's sacrifice, turn back. The discussion of Christ's priesthood is taken up again in chapter 7.

The writer of Hebrews compares the Levitical priesthood—established in the Mosaic covenantal administration—and the priesthood exercised by our Lord. He begins by sketching the duty of the priesthood, which he says is to be the representative of men concerning the things that pertain to God. The Levitical priesthood, he says, can deal gently with sinners because they have their own sins and so must offer sacrifices for themselves as well as the people.

He then states that the priesthood is not a self-appointed office. This fact was valid, he says, concerning Aaron, and the same is true of Christ.

He now comes to the verse, which contains the two citations from the psalms: "So also Christ did not glorify Himself so as to become a high priest, but He who said to Him, 'You are My Son, today I have begotten You'; just as He says also in another *passage*, 'You are a priest forever according to the order of Melchizedek'" (Heb 5:5–6 NASB).

Some may have a problem with these citations regarding the unity of intention between the Old and New Testaments. It may be because of a misunderstanding of the writer's purpose in citing Ps 2:7. Is there evidence in Ps 2:7 (or any other portion of the psalm) that suggests the anointed of the Lord receives the priesthood?

However, I suggest that the writer of Hebrews was not teaching that Ps 2 speaks of the priesthood. Understanding this suggestion requires a close look at the writer's argument and how he introduces both citations.

As we have seen, the writer said that the priesthood is not an office that any man enters according to his initiative. If Christ "did not glorify himself to become high priest, then who was it who did cause Him to become the high priest? It was the One who said about Jesus, 'You are my Son; today I have begotten you'" (Heb 5:5). This same speaker said in another place in the psalms—namely, Ps 110:4—"You are a priest forever after the order of Melchizedek" (NASB). Thus, the writer uses Ps 2:7 to identify the one who appoints and who is appointed, but he uses Ps 110:4 to show the specific office his Anointed is assigned. In other words, he is saying that the speaker is the same in both psalms, and the One to whom he speaks is also the same.

One might also argue that in the declaration concerning Sonship in Ps 2, the psalmist has shown the qualification that the Lord's Anointed possesses to be given the priesthood in Ps 110. Psalm 2:7 speaks not to David but David's Lord, and he possessed Sonship according to the mediatorial significance of the incarnation.

Moving to the citations of Ps 110:4 in chapter 7, the writer makes two distinct points as he praises the superiority of the priesthood of Jesus Christ to the Aaronic. The first point is that Jesus's priesthood finds its basis in the eternal character of the One who holds the office in contrast to the qualification of ancestral descent. The second point is that God's oath confirms the priesthood of Jesus Christ.

According to the first point, we understand that the requirement of the Jewish priesthood is based upon descent, which implies one generation taking the place of another. This circumstance is why the Aaronic priesthood is inferior: Aaron died, and all his descendants are subject to death.

Therefore, the priesthood based on that continuous descent is inferior to Christ's eternal priesthood. "And this is clearer still, if another priest arises according to the likeness of Melchizedek, who has become *such* not on the basis of a law of physical requirement, but according to the power of an indestructible life. For it is attested *of Him*, 'You are a priest forever according to the order of Melchizedek'" (Heb 7:15–17 NASB).

The writer discusses the second point that an oath confirmed the priesthood of Jesus in verses 20 and 21. The Aaronic priests became priests without an oath, "for they indeed became priests without an oath, but He with an oath through the One who said to Him, 'The Lord has sworn and will not change His mind, "You are a priest forever"'" (Heb 7:21 NASB).

Any discrepancy between the intention of the writer of Hebrews and the psalmist at these points must be manufactured. Moreover, the manufactured discrepancy would receive credence only because of prejudice among scholars that every prophecy in the psalms must have at least a partial reference to someone or something in the psalmist's context. This suggestion by liberal scholars is ushered out of court because the something applicable in the writer's context is faith explicitly directed to God's promised Messiah upon which the hope of salvation depends. Nevertheless, there can be no alternative suggestion for claims the writer of Hebrews made for Ps 110:4.

Conclusion

In the previous three chapters, I have dealt with the writers of the New Testament as they have used Old Testament quotations. In the face of both believing and unbelieving scholarship that the New Testament usage is often novel and has little to do with the original intention of the text, I have tried to show otherwise.

As we deal with these matters, we should *recognize* that there is no *objective* starting point—that is, without presuppositions—from which we may begin. You cannot rightly view the Bible from a neutral standpoint, and no one approaches the Bible in truth with such a viewpoint. Those who claim to have such a neutral and unbiased attitude toward Scripture would probably be ignorant of the teaching of both Testaments and have no grounds to form an opinion on the subject.

The conclusions drawn from such a starting place would be essentially worthless from the point of view of my thesis. These conclusions could scarcely be helpful on either side that they might fall, and that would say little about a volume whose intrinsic worth is doubted if it showed harmony and consistency. If the conclusion was one of disharmony, doubt could still be placed upon it because divine inspiration was ignored.

The fact is that the view in which one approaches the Bible is of immense importance to any question that concerns it. The Bible does not come to humanity as a beggar with its hands out asking for tolerant acceptance, but it comes with claims of divine authority and demands obedience. In effect, the individual who says to the Bible, "Prove yourself to me," has already denied the Bible's authority by subjecting it to his own.

The Bible is self-authenticating because the Holy Spirit who inspired it is a real and living person. He also vindicates his work to the reader in its pages and in the hearts and minds of the people he has regenerated. The failure to perceive the Spirit's presence is not a sign of neutral objectivity but the sign of someone who has resisted the Spirit's work. When Eli instructed Samuel on how to respond when God called to him, he did not say to Samuel to cross-question the speaker as to his credentials; instead, he told Samuel to say, "Speak Lord, for your servant is a hearer" (1 Sam 3:9)!

8

Our Approach to Scripture and the Religion of Ancient Israel and Its Precursors: Part 1

Introduction—Expecting the Unexpected

The so-titled father of Latin Christianity, Tertullian, is famously reported to have written, "I believe because it is absurd." Nevertheless, Gerald Lewis Bray suggests that this is a misquotation of Tertullian's words, and what he actually wrote was, "It is credible because it is not fitting." In whatever manner one renders Tertullian's words into English, what he appears to reference is the same idea that the apostle Paul in 1 Corinthians called "the foolishness of God" (1:25 NASB).[1]

If we acknowledge that God says in Isaiah, "For my thoughts are not your thoughts, nor are my ways your ways" (Isa 55:8–9 NASB), then we should expect in his revelation many things that do not conform to the neat contours of human reason. Indeed, God is not irrational, but he may be superrational. Incomprehensibility is among those perfections that we call the attributes of God. Is it not reasonable to expect that the unfolding of his revelation to us will contain unexpected matters regarding theology, history, and culture?

1. Bray, *Holiness and God*, 159n36. The note reads as follows: "In fact, Tertullian never used the expression; see De Carn. Chr. 5.4; *credibile est, quia ineptum est.* On the origin of the phrase, see A. Vaccari, '*Credo quia absurdum. Chi l'ha detto?*', *Scritti di erudizione e di filologia.*"

Comparative religions as a subject often assumes that there is a lowest common denominator to all religions. It further believes that individual religions developed according to the history of a particular people group and their cultural peculiarities as a starting point. The narrative suggests this is the progress of all religions, including that of the Hebrews.

In the case of the Hebrews, some would concede that part of the historical and cultural development was their encounter with the idea of ethical monotheism as the purest form of religion. Through this development, they developed a relationship with the being known as God.

These views, including the one that acknowledges the religion of Israel in its development as superior to others, have one thing in common. They take the position of contemporary and civilized humanity that judges the past from their current vantage point. When one uses the term *judge* in this instance, his interest is not solely, or even primarily, of ethical or moral judgments. Instead, the present becomes the standard by which we judge history and culture as to their place in the evolutionary climb from primitive ideas to modern/postmodern thought.

This assumption implies that any thought of the uniqueness of Israel's religion as distinct from the rest of the world is erroneous. Religions must progress in this way because this is what historical/sociological reasoning says always happens.

Expecting the unexpected is an antidote to this perspective. The revelation of the God who transcends human reason will not mirror the self-generated religious ideas of the rest of the world. The unbeliever and skeptic expect the mirror image, so naturally, they find it. To them, the only antithesis that matters is the antithesis between what is long past and what is present. However, if ancient Israel was the people of God's choice, as the Bible testifies, then the last thing they ought to be is a carbon copy of their pagan neighbors. YHWH's judgment fell upon them when they fell into that same error.

What Is at Stake?

Why is it essential that there be a close relationship between Old Testament and New Testament religion? Why is it important to understand this relationship in more than sequential terms? Why should Reformed and Bible-believing Christians care? The answer to these questions is that a self-generated, evolutionary religion would destroy the idea of the one way of salvation.

The people of Israel (and Judah) were real people. They were not cardboard characters moving through mythological stories to teach a moral or spiritual lesson that may be relevant to God's people today. Each possessed a rational soul that would spend eternity in either blessedness or woe. Moreover, their eternal future depended upon the religion that they practiced. If they could obtain that eternal blessedness by adherence to a religion essentially different from ours, then the idea that there is only one way of salvation is false. In that case, the immutable God has set before fallen humanity essentially different terms of relating to him depending upon the epoch of history when they live.

If this is true, it is no wonder modern and postmodern people recoil from the idea of an exclusive religion. If there was another way in the past, why shouldn't there be another way now? Suppose the people of Israel could gain salvation by sincere adherence to the forms, rites, and ceremonies of religion like the religions of their neighbors. Why should there be an exclusivity today focused upon an entirely different religion?

Our discussion extends beyond forms, rites, and ceremonies. It must question how the saints of the Old Testament were saved. When Peter and John said to the council, "And in none other is there salvation: for neither is there any other name under heaven, that is given among men, wherein we must be saved" (Acts 4:12 NASB), were they making a statement that was only then becoming true? To put the question even more pointedly, is Jesus the Christ, the Messiah of the Old Testament promise? If he is not, we ought to find a more appropriate title for a new kind of Savior. Indeed, in that case, the title *Christ* should also be removed from him. Yet, we cannot do this because the New Testament gives him this title.

Setting the Boundaries

Before one begins this discussion in earnest, it is necessary to set some boundaries. This action is essential because of the previous statements about expecting the unexpected. There should be no misunderstanding; expecting the unexpected is not an endorsement of irrationality. God is incomprehensible, and the Bible speaks the truth when it says that his "ways are past finding out" (Rom 11:33 KJV). Nevertheless, the Bible does not proclaim a God who is irrational.

This doctrine is not a judgment made about the Bible; it is the teaching of the Bible. "God is light," we are told, "and in Him is no darkness at all" (1 John 1:5, 7 NASB). He hates sin and loves righteousness. These statements set logical antitheses before us and are true of God. They rule out the possibility that the Bible is an escape from reason. They also forbid the idea that the God of the Bible is a purely irrational ruler.

This understanding is not the only reason, however, for setting boundaries. The standpoint from which one writes as a Bible-believing Christian, places some methodologies, suggestions, and assumptions out of bounds. What we say here is partly based upon the previous insistence that a so-called neutral viewpoint is impossible. For example, suppose one begins from a starting position that says there may be no God. In that case, he will never come to the viewpoint of Tertullian, who wrote, "And this is the crowning guilt of men, that they will not recognize One, of whom they cannot possibly be ignorant."[2] The supposition that God may not exist is incompatible with the belief that one "cannot possibly be ignorant" of him. Starting at the agnostic position, one must say of Tertullian's theistic conclusion, "You cannot get there from here."

Moreover, a discussion with no boundaries may make the debate a little like trying to hit a small bull's-eye from one hundred yards with the discharge of a twelve-gauge shotgun. Limits to the discussion keep it on track and provide some protection from following dead-end rabbit trails.

The first boundary that we wish to set mandates an approach to Scripture as the revelation of God. This understanding is a given and not a hypothesis that we must prove. Some may criticize this as unscientific. Nonetheless, it is necessary. When anyone approaches the Bible as an authority that must prove itself, it is then a case of a human being placing himself as a judge of the credentials of God's word. His revelation, contrariwise, is the judge of humankind.[3] It is as if a litigant coming into a court has a right to decide whether he will or will not recognize the duly appointed judge on the bench. There is One who judges and one whose case is judged, and he errs if he attempts to reverse things.

Some maintain that such an approach is unscholarly and unscientific. E. J. Young, nevertheless, shows that this is the only way to proceed. He says this:

2. Tertullian, *Apology*, ch. 17.

3. For an excellent exposition of this matter, see Young, *Book of Isaiah*, 3:189–208.

> Indeed, people may study the Bible rightly in one way only. They must approach it as those who have submitted their entire being to God and come to His Word ready to listen and obey all He has to say. The alternative view erects a daysman [an umpire] between the Word and ourselves to judge the Word. Since man is the one to erect the daysman, he is, in fact, no genuine daysman but merely a creation of the human mind. Because the Bible is God's very Word and revelation, any daysman who stands between it and man is, in reality, a daysman between God and man. Nevertheless, there is no superior to God. Anyone claiming to be His judge is actually claiming to be God.[4]

Some Bible-believing Christians, recognizing that skeptics do not approach the Bible in this fashion, will sideline their personal faith commitment and approach the Scriptures with these skeptics as if the Bible's authority was a mere hypothesis. The words of professor Young apply in this situation also. Whether or not the umpire that we might choose is favorable enough to the claims to treat the Bible as a working hypothesis, it is still an attempt to set human wisdom as the arbiter of truth. God claims this position for himself alone, and no others need to apply!

The second boundary is *to not* allow evolutionary assumptions to seep into the discussion. The theory concerning the development of biological life generally teaches that life progresses slowly from the beginning with an organism that is very simple to ever-more complex organisms over time. As a theory of cosmic origins, evolution is unbiblical. However, this evolutionary plan of the simple to the complex has also seeped into other areas of study. One can speak of evolution in the realm of history and sociology, as well as other branches of human endeavor.

Biblical studies are not immune to this seepage, in general, or in the study of the religion of Israel in particular. This fact is evident in the German school of *Religionsgeschichte* of the nineteenth and early twentieth centuries. Sadly, there is also evidence of it within orthodox scholarship. This perspective claims that religions naturally progress from the simple, both in terms of rituals and beliefs, to the complex. Therefore, this journey is what they expect in the development of the religion of the Hebrews.

We must be careful. As a general principle, if we believe that we will find a specific pattern in our historical research, it is not surprising if we see it. If I convince myself that every cloud contains the image of Abraham

4. Young, *Book of Isaiah*, 3:194.

Lincoln, it is not surprising that I suddenly find Abraham Lincoln's face staring at me from every cloud.

Let me briefly state the dangers of evolutionary presuppositions in this regard. There is the danger of treating Israel's religion as a member of the more prominent family of the ancient Near East religions. There is also the danger of seeing its progress as the natural outworking of evolutionary pressures. There is the danger of looking at things that result from bald-faced spiritual rebellion and unbelief as nothing more than the normal state of spiritual development reached by that time. The possibility also exists of concluding that the past can shine a light upon the future but that the future cannot illuminate the past. A person can erroneously believe that certain so-called New Testament doctrines do not find a place in Israel's ancient religion. Some reach this conclusion—not because of the different covenantal administrations—but because of alleged religious and theological incapacities.

The next thing to mention is the need to make cautious use of the concept of continuity and discontinuity. There is no question that both can exist as one compares the revelation found in the Old Testament and the New. However, scholars have a temptation and a tendency to maximize the discontinuity and minimize the continuity. This practice is a mistake because they often conclude that the Christianity of the New Testament is a significantly different religion from that of the patriarchs, Moses, and the prophets.

Systematic theological concerns may suffer at this point. Reformed and Presbyterian scholars may confess that there is only one covenant of grace in the Old and New Testaments, though with different administrations. Yet, in practice, they may speak of the Old Testament religion as if it contained few of the Christian doctrines found in the New Testament. They make the former confession an act of ecclesiastical orthodoxy, while in the product of the daily work they assert as matters of scholarly necessity the omission of references to so-called New Testament doctrines in the Old Testament.

For example, some scholars maintain that ancient Israel had no true conception of life after death, to say nothing of the resurrection. If that is true, how does the salvation to which they looked resemble the salvation that Paul expressed: "To live is Christ and to die is gain" (Phil 1:21 NASB)? Paul tells his readers in 1 Corinthians that without the hope of the resurrection, Christians are "of all men most to be pitied" (15:19b NASB). Why didn't the people of ancient Israel consider that they were of all men most to be pitied? Wouldn't this be true if God had revealed nothing concerning the resurrection to them? An unknown promise is a promise that offers no comfort!

Next, one must treat seriously subtle signals in the word of God. Psalm 23, for example, concludes with the words, "And I will dwell in the house of the Lord forever" (v. 6b). Does this mean that the psalmist only pledges to spend the remaining days of his life in the temple? This thought is a possible rendering when you treat the words as hyperbole. With this interpretation, forever means as long as I live. What if it means quite literally forever? Goodness and mercy will follow me all the days of my life (in other words, as long as I live), and in addition to this, I will dwell in the house of the Lord in eternity.

Another example of subtle signals in God's word that suggest continuity in the Old Testament with what God would later reveal in the New Testament is from Luke 24. This is the narrative of Cleopas and his colleague on the road to Emmaus. Luke says that Emmaus was seven miles distant from Jerusalem, a journey on foot of some hours. He also tells us that Jesus met them on that road and walked with them. One doesn't know precisely when this occurred, but Luke informs his readers that it was before they arrived at the village. When Jesus was with the two disciples, Luke says that beginning with Moses and all the prophets, Jesus told them the things concerning himself from the Scriptures. This instruction appears to be a somewhat lengthy explanation, not a few disjointed references to isolated passages.

I conclude the discussion of subtle signs by looking at John 8:56: "Your father *Abraham rejoiced to see My day, he saw it and was glad*" (NASB, emphasis mine). We should not reduce our Lord's statement to a suggestion that Abraham only had some vague understanding that the promises given him went beyond himself. Jesus's words require much more than that. Jesus says Abraham saw and rejoiced in the future that revealed Jesus Christ.

There is a fifth boundary I want to cover in discussing the religion of ancient Israel. It is the genuine need to distinguish between alleged cultural and historical ignorance and covenantal unbelief. The former means that ignorant people could not comprehend New Testament doctrines, and the latter means that these advanced doctrines were misunderstood because of Israel's unbelief and rebellion.

On the one hand, there is a supposition that it is ignorance and disability with which we primarily deal in studying the Old Testament. It leads us to suspect that God would not expect Old Testament Israel to understand New Testament ideas such as a multipersonal God. Therefore, any suggestion that the concept appears in the Old Testament must be ruled inadmissible.

On the other hand, ancient Israel is often presented in the Old Testament as a *stiff-necked people*, rebelling again and again against God's clear revelation. If such a phenomenon explains Israel's failure to obey the commandments, is it not reasonable to believe that it demonstrates their inability to consider the promises as well?

I must draw a further boundary. This boundary marks the distinction between the rites and ceremonies of the Old Testament religion contrasted with their essence. The outward form of the Old Testament temple (and tabernacle) worship was quite distinct from the simplicity of the worship of the New Testament church.

Does this mean that there is no continuity between the two? By no means! Anyone who reads the book of Hebrews knows that the writer makes no secret of the significant differences between the old covenant's rites and the new covenant's forms. His use of the terms *old* and *new* signifies the old administration of the covenant of grace and the new administration of the covenant of grace. As we have previously seen, the same writer also bases his Christology squarely upon the teaching of the Old Testament.

Covenant theology teaches us that since the sin of our first parents, God's people have been under the covenant of grace. Few, if any, Reformed and Presbyterian scholars would disagree. Nonetheless, we are required to go deeper.

Salvation is by grace through faith in Christ, which is true of salvation for the New Testament believers, who look back at Jesus Christ as he appeared in "the fullness of the time" (Gal 4:4 NASB). Old Testament saints also looked forward to Christ as promised in the law, the prophets, and the writings. Grace, faith, and Christ are inseparable in true salvation. If faith is a work (or works replace faith), grace disappears, and any salvation ceases to be *of grace*. Likewise, it presents a different kind of salvation if you replace Christ as the particular object of faith with something else. There is no unified covenant of grace if there is a different kind of salvation in the Old Testament from that of the New.

The last thing I need to mention in setting boundaries for the discussion is that one must remember who he is. One approaches this discussion aware that he is a Christian, united to his Savior by faith. He is one whose salvation depends upon the atoning sacrifice of Jesus Christ, and he understands that this is the only possible way of salvation since the fall of humanity into sin.

This truth is the only safe standpoint from which to approach any biblical inquiry. It is undoubtedly true we ought to expect the unexpected, but that must be defined from the perspective of belief and not unbelief. The teaching of Scripture is the teaching of the God who is incomprehensible. Therefore, we should not expect it to be formed by human reason, and we do not expect the Bible's teaching to be a mere echo of man-made religion.

The Religion of Ancient Israel

I must begin this section with a disclaimer. There is no claim that the religion in Israel of the Old Testament was identical in its rites and ceremonies to the religion presented in the New Testament. The very name *New Testament* implies that there is something new. Thus, the discussion will center on whether the relation between the Testaments is between that which is old and new or something entirely different. Is it a matter of promise and fulfillment or two entirely dissimilar religions?

In the confines of this chapter and the following, I intend to briefly show that the religion revealed by God to his people is fundamentally the same under the guise of different rites and ceremonies. The Almighty has not provided the New Testament believer an entirely different way of salvation than was available for the saints of the Old.

There is a lens through which I will view the subject.[5] The oft-repeated saying, "The New Testament is in the Old Testament concealed, and the Old Testament is in the New Testament revealed," describes the proper lens one uses. This understanding prioritizes the New Testament and suggests the dominance of the person of Christ, not only in the New Testament but

5. There is no choice of whether a reader will use a lens. Without some guiding principle in the organization of the biblical data, one confronts a mass of unrelated facts incapable of interpretation. The history of religions school of a century past indeed had a lens through which it viewed the subject. The question is whether the lens is biblically justified. In his insistence that the Scriptures testified of him, our Lord critiqued his opponents for using the wrong lens in their study of the Old Testament.

also in the Old Testament. I have dealt with these issues already in chapter 2.

If the New Testament were merely a revival or revitalization of the Old Testament in the manner of the prophets of the Old Testament, then it would be justifiable to prioritize the Old Testament in the discussion. We would study the Old Testament to discover its essential themes and principles, asking how the New Testament called people back to these moorings. On the other hand, if we correctly see that the New Testament is the goal the Old Testament aims for, then the New Testament must have priority in the discussion. The New Testament would appear as the flowering of true religion, and its dominant themes and principles will be sought in the revelation given in the Old Testament.

Given this understanding that the focal point of the New Testament is the person of Jesus Christ as the ultimate revelation of the triune God, he will appear as dominant not only for New Testament writers but also for those of the Old Testament. The person of Christ permeates the Old Testament, and he is not there as an intrusion.

The specific interest in this discussion is the nature of the religion of ancient Israel. According to biblical revelation, Israel is not an entity that hangs in midair without foundation. Moses did not invent the faith of the Israelites as they came out of Egypt. Therefore, we must examine the foundation of pre-Israelite covenantal religion.

The books of Exodus through Deuteronomy, which delineate the Old Testament Law, have Genesis as their background. In Exodus, we are told that a Pharaoh arose "who knew not Joseph" (1:8 KJV), but that did not mean that Joseph, his family, and his ancestors did not exist. The Old Testament does not have its origin at Sinai; there were places "in the beginning" at the Creation.

Since those who believe in covenant theology consider the covenant in the garden of Eden as different from the one instituted after the fall, there may be a presumption that the pre-fall religion was completely different from the religion of the covenant of grace. However, we may overstate this presumption. Overstatement occurs when it suggests that the way of salvation encompasses all of religion. There was a different way of obtaining eternal life under the covenant of works (or covenant of life). Nevertheless, the conception that salvation comprises the whole of religion is not sound.

To say that the whole of religion is one's own salvation makes religion man-centered. As a now-deceased friend insisted, the heart of true faith is having God for God's sake, not for what he can do for you. Therefore, true religion must include the object of worship that it proclaims. God is the object of worship and fellowship in both the faith of the covenant of works (pre-fall) and the religion of the covenant of grace (post-fall). Adam in his innocence and the sincere Christian of today can unite in declaring with the Westminster Shorter Catechism, the chief end of man "is to glorify God, and to enjoy him forever."[6]

In addition to the same object of worship, pre-fall and post-fall religions have other similarities. Both religions are founded upon God's sovereign activity concerning man. The covenant of works is no more self-generated than the covenant of grace. Moreover, the principle of grace is not absent in the covenant of works. Even though Adam and Eve were created free of sin, God owed them nothing. The question, "Does not the potter have a right over the clay?" (Rom 9:21 NASB), says nothing about the moral character of the clay, and it bases its pointedness upon the creative rights of the potter.

I am not arguing that pre-fall religion is precisely the same as post-fall religion. Nor am I saying that the post-fall religion of the Old Testament is the same as the New Testament religion. I am merely suggesting that, even at this point, one cannot find complete discontinuity.

I have an additional reason for stressing commonalities between Eden's religion and the religion of the Bible as a whole. The claim of the covenant of works continues as an obligation to everyone outside the covenant of grace. God still requires of them "personal, perfect, and perpetual obedience"[7] to him.

Moreover, the obedience of Jesus Christ under this works covenant laid the foundation of the covenant of grace. God in Christ did not annul his claim for perfect obedience; he fulfilled it and offered its benefits to those united to Jesus Christ by faith.

I briefly state another reason to stress continuity rather than discontinuity. Human beings do not enter the covenant of grace by their initiative, and this circumstance was true of the first pair and also of their posterity. Almighty God chooses to which covenant one belongs.

This state of affairs appears in two ways. First, in the promise that underlies the covenant of grace God announces in the curse that he pronounces upon the serpent immediately after the sin of Adam. Secondly, the

6. Westminster Standards, Shorter Catechism, Q/A 1.

7. Westminster Standards, Larger Catechism, Q/A 20.

Lord provided coverings of animal skins to the fallen couple at his initiative, and this image removed the shame of nakedness. An attempt to establish the covenant of grace by human initiative would be mere presumption.

Therefore, we may see that the two covenants are linked together. Yes, they provide distinctly different ways to eternal life; however, God erects the covenant of grace out of the ruin of the covenant of works. The covenant of grace is a religion based upon God's sovereign initiative and man's response of faith.

According to Genesis, the time that stretches from Adam to Noah is only briefly covered relative to the centuries in which it took place. This circumstance precludes any detailed analysis of the character of the religion practiced by Adam and his descendants until the flood, but I may note certain factors:

1. The naming of Cain may well indicate Eve's hope that the child she was bearing would be the fulfillment of the promise of a Savior to crush the serpent's head.[8]
2. The sacrifices given by Cain and Abel may indicate a knowledge of God's claim upon humanity for sacrificial worship.
3. The acceptance of Abel's sacrifice, taken from his flocks, perhaps signifies the need for worship based upon the shedding of blood.
4. Tracing two distinct genealogical lines, one notably ungodly and one presumably godly, develops the concept of an antithesis from early on.
5. The translation of Enoch, the seventh from Adam, signifies a religion that had a central part of fellowship between the human worshiper and God.
6. Grace is illustrated by Noah's faith in the promise of God to provide for him a way of escape from the terrible judgment upon the sin and wickedness of the human race.

8. Many commentators make this suggestion. The interpretation relies on a variety of factors. First, there is the proximity in the text of Eve's announcement of the child's name to the promise of the previous chapter. Then, the text's wording, "I have acquired," is another factor since this may indicate that she considered this birth to be a particular gift from the Lord, not merely the natural course of events concerning the procreation of children. A third thing mentioned is the grammar that would cause the text to run literally, "I have acquired a man, even the Lord." The translators have inserted "the help of," and the phrase is in the original.

7. The division of animals for inclusion into the ark: seven pairs of clean animals and one pair of unclean, suggests that there was at that early time a need to emphasize the same condition that is found later in the Mosaic economy.
8. God required sacrifices of thanksgiving after the flood.

Remembering the inability to make a detailed analysis of the religion established in the antediluvian world, we may still ask what conclusions we can draw from the observations above. It is necessary to remember the fourth item on the list as we do so. There have always been both true and false religions, so this most likely was the case in the world's early history. It is hardly supportable to believe that the murderous Lamech was a worshiper of the living and true God. Contrariwise, it is impossible to think that Enoch was not.

Among the godly, the object of worship was God. Except among the prejudiced, there is nothing to indicate that they worshiped him not as the triune God. The first human pair in their state of innocence fellowshipped with God face to face. Why would one assume he did not reveal himself according to his triune nature? Fallen humanity may have needed progressive revelation, but that says nothing concerning the condition in the garden. Did Adam and Eve forget the revelation God previously gave to them? Were they as unsuited as later generations to understand the import of the statement, "Let us make man in our image" (Gen 1:26 KJV)? Even if one supposes, as per Charles Hodge, that there is only a bare hint of the Trinity contained in the plural, may one assume the unfallen intellect of Adam was able to connect the dots?[9]

A second matter to consider is the faith that was an integral part of this religion. Eve demonstrated it in naming her firstborn; her words strongly imply that faith had as its object God's promise of One who was to come to crush the serpent's head. Abel displayed faith in the sacrifice that he brought (Gen 4:4). One may infer that Enoch's life was characterized by

9. There is a curious tendency to treat the words as if they were the product of Moses (or whomever the interpreter imagines the writer to be), placing them on the lips of the Lord. In this case, the writer's knowledge of the nature of the Godhead would set a limit upon what the words could be interpreted to mean. Nonetheless, such is not the case. These words are not the product of Moses's intellect producing a statement of theology that he was composing under the inspiration of the Holy Spirit. This knowledge was received from the Holy Spirit, reporting what was said when no human being was present. It is, therefore, not a question of Moses's understanding of the language, "Let us," but it is a matter of what the triune God meant when he said it.

faith as he "walked with God" (Gen 5:24). Noah responded in faith to God's direction concerning the flood and the building of an ark.

In the third place, there is a clear understanding that the worship of God was connected to sacrifice. Neither is it too far a cast to suggest that acceptance with God required the shedding of blood. As far as we know, at the time of Abel's sacrifice, humanity had not been permitted to consume the flesh of animals. Noah's sacrifice after the flood confirms perhaps the relationship between worship and sacrifice (Gen 8:20).

Another matter is the principle of holiness, displayed in several ways. The sacrifice of Abel was accepted, unlike the sacrifice of Cain. Was this because Abel's sacrifice acknowledged the holiness of God? Enoch's translation into God's presence is perhaps a witness to the holiness of his life compared to his contemporaries. The separation of animals between clean and unclean in the time of Noah is a display of holiness, which has separated the holy from the profane or common.

Moreover, in all these indications, one is struck by the theocentric initiation of the matters involved. It is God who causes Eve to acquire a man-child. God determines what sacrifice is acceptable to him and what state of the heart is acceptable in bringing a sacrifice. It is God who takes Enoch to himself. One infers that God determines which animals are clean and which are unclean. God pronounces judgment on the wickedness of humankind. He singles out Noah and his immediate family as the objects of his redemption.

This idea brings us to the consideration of grace, where God is sovereign in his dealings with man and where that dealing does not lead to immediate condemnation. That is where grace reigns triumphant. Even when we consider the flood a terrible judgment upon the human race, Noah and his family stand out as a trophy of that grace.

There is no difference in principle between this religion and the more detailed exhibition of ancient Israel's religion. I am also of the opinion that there is no difference of principle in the religion of the New Testament church.

The biblical record is even briefer between Noah and Abraham than the record of the time between Adam and Noah. Others have written much of the difference between the administration of the Noahic covenant and later administrations of the covenant of grace. Our interest is in the similarities, particularly with the religion in effect among God's people.

The Bible says comparatively little of true religion after the lifetime of Noah. Nevertheless, there are some hints concerning Noah after the flood from which we might learn. In addition to this, the book of Job deals with a worshiper of God who is not a descendant of Abraham and who is either of Abraham's time or earlier. These matters give us some indications of true religion during this time.

After coming out of the ark, Noah's immediate activity was to sacrifice some of the clean animals. However, there is no evidence that these were anything other than sacrifices of thanksgiving. Additionally, God enters into a covenant with Noah and all living creatures that he will never again destroy the earth by a flood. As a sign, the Lord sets the rainbow in the sky. The promise here in the covenant with Noah is given without condition. As long as the earth endures, so shall remain seedtime and harvest, summer and winter (see Gen 8).

The religion established by this covenant was not one of works to bring the promise to pass. Nonetheless, moral obligation existed under its terms. This fact appears in two ways. First, as God gave mankind the liberty to eat the flesh of animals, there was the stipulation that meat should be eaten without its blood (Gen 9:1–6). Notably, this prohibition continued in the Mosaic law and the decree of the Jerusalem Council in Acts 15.

The second way moral obligation appears is linked to the first, but additional significance is given to the shedding of blood. It is the command that human beings in reprisal should also kill anyone who murderously sheds a human's blood. This command includes both animals, who might slay a human being, and other human beings (see Lev 17:10–16). In this, the sixth commandment of the Mosaic law is anticipated.

Other ethical issues are noted. These are found in the narrative surrounding Noah's drunkenness and the different reactions of his sons to it. The text does not overtly declare this act on Noah's part to be a sin. Nevertheless, both Ham's unrighteous response and Shem and Japheth's righteous response imply that Noah's action was a display of moral failing. Ham mocks his father's behavior while the two other brothers, as it were, cover their father's shame (Gen 9:22–27).[10]

To find clues outside the Pentateuch of the religion that existed among the godly before the call of Abram, one must go to the book of Job. The Bible tells us Job lived in the land of Uz, and the name Uz is also found in the descendants of Shem (Job 1:1). Whether Job was a contemporary of the

10. Notably, nakedness is used in Gen 3 to indicate the shame brought forth by sin.

patriarchs or lived before them, Scripture undoubtedly represents him as a worshiper of the living and true God. What can one learn from Job about the religion that he practiced?

The first thing one learns about him is that he was "blameless and upright," as the ESV puts it. Two other characteristics were that he feared God and turned away from evil (Job 1:1). The first of the two couplets reflects a moral rectitude in the world's sight. The second couplet speaks of a righteousness that is internal and combines a reverence for God with the hatred of evil.

These descriptions of Job are repeated, but the second time they come from the mouth of YHWH as he directs Satan's attention to Job (Job 1:8). The fact that God uses these words himself shows that the moral standard that Job was using to control his attitudes and behavior had God's approval. It is what Reformed theology calls the law of God written upon the heart.

In addition, we learn of a place for sacrifices in Job's religious life. Because of the possibility of his sons and daughter cursing God during their frequent feasts, Job habitually offered sacrifices to God on their behalf (Job 1:5). These sacrifices may be called substitutionary, and Job performs the function of a priest on behalf of his household. He resembles the patriarchs Abraham, Isaac, and Jacob in this situation.

Job's sacrifices appear to have the Lord's approval because God rebukes Job's three friends for their presumptuous speech about YHWH, and he directs them to bring bullocks and rams to Job that he might sacrifice them. In addition, God tells these three men that Job will intercede for them to prevent his judgment upon them (Job 42:8). Thus, prayer is a part of Job's religion, a feature God commands.

One must not consider the religion of Job (nor any other person) apart from its theology. Job has faith; he trusts in God when all is taken away from him. His response is, "The Lord gave and the Lord has taken away. Blessed be the name of the Lord" (1:21 NASB), and, "Shall we receive good and not evil from the Lord?" (2:10 NASB). When the dreadful disease comes upon him, he stoutly refuses to "curse God and die" (2:9 NASB).

Moreover, Job's faith and trust are not simply in God as the sovereign dispenser of good and evil. Chapter 19 is key to this understanding. He addresses God as his redeemer (*goali*)[11] and that this redeemer will at last stand upon the earth (*weaharown al apar yaqum*, v. 25).[12] Job's theology

11. Bible Hub, "1350. Gaal."

12. Bible Hub, "314. Acharon"; "5921. Al"; "6083. Aphar"; "6965. Qum."

also relates this event of the distant future to himself. The language in which this is stated has been rendered differently by various translators. Many have it as, "And, after my skin is destroyed, yet in my flesh I shall see God." Conversely, others translated it as, "And after my skin is destroyed, yet apart from my flesh I shall see God" (v. 26).

The difference here is whether the preposition *from* is to be seen in the sense of *from the standpoint of* or *apart from*. In either case, we see in Job a testimony to some manner of life after the destruction of the body. In the former case, it would be a belief in a bodily resurrection, and in the latter case, merely a belief in the immortality of the spirit.

The significance of the difference in translation is not small. The question for those translating the words "apart from my flesh I will see God" is the reason for their translation. Is it due to the Hebrew syntax and grammar? Or is it because Job was unable, given his historical and cultural setting, to come to any belief in a resurrection of the body?

Nevertheless, whichever translation one prefers of Job 19:25–26, Job's theology contained hope in the afterlife. Moreover, this hope was tied to his faith in God as his redeemer, for the verses make clear that the Redeemer who will stand at last upon the earth is God. Therefore, given the picture of One who stands upon the earth, it is within the realm of possibility that Job had some seminal understanding of the incarnation of deity.

Looking at Job and his religious understanding brings the discussion to the period of the patriarchs: Abraham, Isaac, and Jacob. This is an excellent place to break the discussion and take it up again in the following chapter.

9

Our Approach to Scripture and the Religion of Ancient Israel and Its Precursors: Part 2

The Religion of the Patriarchs

Previously, we surveyed the religion in place before Israel appeared as a distinct nation. Though we could describe the time of Abraham, Isaac, and Jacob in the same manner, the people of Israel regarded this period of the patriarchs as a distinct part of their history as a distinct people.

As we approach the period of the patriarchs, it is necessary to understand that there is no evidence that the patriarchs crafted their religion from the surrounding pagan background. Some of them fell into pagan practices upon occasion, but this was a defection from the faith that God had given them.

Because the nation of Israel descended from the patriarchs and their religion was undoubtedly divine in its origin, we return to the question we have been asking: Is the religion of the patriarchs essentially the same religion of Jesus and his apostles? Was there a fundamentally different way the patriarchs found acceptance with God other than the way presented in the New Testament?

Regarding the patriarchs, at least Abraham, we do not limit our view to conjectures drawn from the Old Testament texts. Instead, one finds insights from the apostle Paul, writing under the inspiration of the Holy Spirit: "For, if Abraham was justified of works, he has boasting, but not before God. The

Scripture says, 'And Abraham believed God, and he accounted it to him as righteousness'" (Rom 4:2–3).

It is not an uncertain text from which we read that Abraham's justification was by faith. Undoubtedly Paul intended to teach that very truth. Therefore, if we maintain that Abraham's standing before God was on some basis other than his faith in God and God's promise, we suggest more than a different religion for Abraham. We would be suggesting that Paul in Rom 4 was writing for no purpose.

It is not only in the area of justification that Abraham's religion resembles the religion set forth by the apostle Paul. There is a resemblance in the area of sanctification as well. In Gen 18:19, we read, "For I have known him, to the end that he may command his children and his household after him, that they may keep the way of the [Lord], to do righteousness and justice; to the end that the [Lord] may bring upon Abraham that which he has spoken of him" (ASV). As Rom 8:29 says, "For those he foreknew he also predestined to be conformed to the image of his Son; so that he might be the firstborn among many brethren."

There is unquestionably a precision in the words of the apostle since he wrote in the light of messianic fulfillment. For example, Paul knew that the godliness the Holy Spirit produces is the progressive transformation of the believer into the image of Jesus Christ.

We know Moses received no revelation about this as he wrote Genesis. However, he *had* received the revelation that God's people were to be holy because he, the Lord, was holy (e.g., Lev 11:44). From this, he could learn that the "righteousness and justice" that Abraham and his children were to do *reflected* the character of God. Furthermore, the culmination of the promises given to Abraham was the consummation where the risen Christ stands as the "firstborn among many brethren."

The essence of any religion is not found in its external rituals but the internal relationship between the divine object (or objects of worship) and the worshipers. Suppose two or more expressions of religion have the same essential understanding of justification and sanctification (to use Christian terminology). In that case, we may safely conclude that they are essentially the same religion. This understanding holds regardless of the outward manifestations of ritual and ceremony.

We are not limited to the doctrines of justification and sanctification when examining the religion of Abraham and the other patriarchs. The divine initiative is another factor, as we have already seen. God takes the initiative in its establishment. God approaches Abram and tells him to move from Haran into Canaan (Gen 12:1–7). The establishment of the covenant and its subsequent ratifications are also at YHWH's initiative.

With Isaac, we may also see this initiative from the Lord. Before his birth, the promise was repeatedly given that he would be born to an elderly and barren woman (Gen 17:19; 18:10; 21:1–2; etc.). We see YHWH's provision of the substitute of the ram for the sacrifice of Isaac that God commanded Abraham (Gen 22:12–13). God also approaches Isaac in a time of famine and commands him not to go down with his family to Egypt (Gen 26:1–2).

The Lord said of Jacob's relationship with his older brother, "The elder shall serve the younger" (Gen 25:23 ASV). God appears to him at Bethel to confirm the covenant. YHWH's initiative produces Jacob's promise to give a tenth of his increase to God, and he erects a pillar as an act of worship (Gen 28:10–22). If we may say it reverently, God initiates the wrestling match by the river Jabok (Gen 32:24). Jacob also waits for God's permission before he accedes to Joseph's invitation to move with his family down to Egypt (Gen 46:1–4).

The previously mentioned emphasis on God's initiative is significant because it places a seal of authenticity upon that religion. Man-made religion has the marks of its origin clearly upon it. So it is with true religion; one of the most indelible signs of this is God's initiation. The *call to worship* in Christian worship is more than a ceremonial ritual; it is a reminder that God seeks and calls human beings to himself that we might worship him, and he might give life to us.

The concept of the covenant is the Lord's initiation of the patriarchs' religion and the resultant idea of God calling people into a relationship with him. God tells us the essential characteristic of the divine covenant is, "I will . . . be your God, and you will be my people" (Lev 26:12 NASB).

Much has been expertly written about the covenant, especially by Reformed authors. Nevertheless, it is necessary to point out that, if God enters into a relationship with a people from one time period on the same basis as he established with those from a different period, then the religion that arises will be essentially the same.

God is free to change covenant ritual and ceremony details, as differing circumstances require. This truth does not affect the underlying nature of the covenant or its promises. Neither does it change the essential nature of the religion that arises from the covenant relationship.

The covenant character of patriarchal religion exhibits its gracious character to a great degree. The term *to a great degree* indicates that the religion is of pure grace. Whatever grace in a religion that is not founded in the divinely initiated call to his people cannot be a religion of pure grace. If the religion teaches that the human being must initiate the quest for worship, grace is limited. In manufactured worship, the supposed deity responds to the would-be worshiper; in true religion, human beings react to Almighty God in his sovereign call.

The concept of sacrifice further displays the gracious character of patriarchal religion. The patriarchs habitually erect sacrificial altars at the places of their temporary residences. Throughout Scripture, the concept of sacrifice points to substitutionary atonement for sin. However, there is an example in the time of the patriarchs that goes beyond the relationship between the shedding of blood and the forgiveness of sin. In Gen 15:1–18, YHWH takes upon himself the sanction of his people's violation of the covenant. God ratified his covenant with Abraham in that place, and the slaughtered animals symbolized the ratification. This rite is symbolic of the sanction unleashed in breaking the covenant, but God, not Abraham, in the figure of a flaming torch passed through the separated pieces.

Finally, there is an ethical character in the religion of the patriarchs. We have already met this in Gen 18:19, where God says that Abraham is to teach his children to "keep the way of the Lord" (NASB). The word *way* is used in the Old Testament to express the prescriptive will of God for his people.

Genesis 26:4–5 puts the matter beyond all possible doubt: "I will multiply your descendants as the stars of heaven, and will give your descendants all these lands; and by your descendants, all the nations of the earth shall be blessed, because Abraham obeyed Me and fulfilled his duty to Me, and kept My commandments, My statutes, and My laws" (NASB). Even though the commandments, statutes, and judgments are not explicitly recorded in Genesis, they were made clear to Abraham.

The Religion of Israel from Moses Through Joshua

The Mosaic economy of Israel's religion stretches throughout the entire period of the Old Testament and the intertestamental period. Nevertheless, since the ensuing centuries added elements to Israel's faith that were only embryonic in the time of Moses and Joshua, we will now look specifically at the religion of Israel during that time. I will not examine the minutiae of the covenant in this chapter.

If we consider the ceremonial law that structures the outward form of Israel's religion: the sacrifices of various sorts, the holy days of the feasts, and the high holy day of affliction and fasting—the Day of Atonement—we would see an outward form very different from that of the New Testament religion.

There is certainly an arena where such examination is both legitimate and profitable, but the search for the heart of Old Testament religion is not *in* that place. In that search, the minutiae could obscure the goal of the investigation. To use a somewhat hackneyed expression, one cannot see the forest for the trees.

Another matter should be observed. Not everything of a religious nature among the Israelites is part of the revealed religion that God gave to his people. Stephen, in Acts 7:43, says concerning the people of the exodus, "You also took along the tabernacle of Moloch and the star of your god Rompha, the images which you made to worship" (NASB). Therefore, we notice that some of the people were engaged in active idolatry including worship of the golden calf, even as the LORD delivered them from bondage.

This means that as we investigate the religion of Israel at its beginning as a nation, we must draw distinctions. The contrast must be made between the worship and faith that God instituted and the worship that was the invention of human beings. The mixture of true and false appeared from the nation's beginning, even before they entered the national homeland.

We must exercise another caution in studying the ancient religion of Israel. This caution is the realization that Israel was both a nation *and* the church of the Old Testament. Her existence as a body politic was intertwined with her being a religious community. However, if we treat the two as the same thing, we make a mistake. The distinction between civil and ceremonial law is fundamental and should not be considered an unwarranted Puritan assumption.[1] There are matters in the Pentateuch that are political and do not concern the religious establishment.

There is a sense in which a kind of legalism is proper in a nation for its stability. The laws and statutes lead to social upheaval if wantonly disobeyed. Moreover, disobedience brings dishonor upon the lawbreaker in a society where the laws originate from the God of heaven. Nevertheless,

1. I have in mind here the charge that the division of the law into moral, ceremonial, and judicial is an innovation of the Puritans in the Westminster Assembly.

social well-being is not to be confused with eternal salvation. The presence of a legal system in the Mosaic economy and the exhortations to obedience to that system do not mean that Israel's religion was one of works righteousness.

As in the case of the patriarchs, the Mosaic religion was at God's initiative. This understanding is evident in Exod 3, in which God calls Moses, the fugitive from Pharaoh's wrath, who was keeping his father-in-law's sheep. In addition, some vestiges of patriarchal religion apparently remained in the mind of Moses and other Israelites. For example, the Hebrew midwives disobeyed Pharaoh because they feared God (Exod 1:17). We also learn from the book of Hebrews that his parents hid Moses by faith. He forsook his high position as the son of Pharaoh's daughter also by faith (Heb 11:23–27).

Nevertheless, in general, the Hebrews had adopted much of the religious notions of Egypt. The Lord explicitly informs Moses that he will judge the gods of Egypt and the people of Egypt, which strongly suggests that the pagan gods of Egypt were a snare for the descendants of Abraham, Isaac, and Jacob (Exod 12:12).

We return to the initiative of God, which shows itself in many ways, in addition to the call of Moses. Each time Moses approaches Pharaoh, he does so at YHWH's command. Each of the ten plagues comes with the Lord's determination (see Exod 7–12). The preface to the Ten Commandments announces that the Lord their God brought (and bought) them out of slavery and bondage (Exod 20:1–2).

Yet, when we speak of God's initiative, precisely of whom do we speak? At first, this may appear to be a strange question, but let us return to Exod 3. The One who appears to Moses in verse 2 is called "the angel of the Lord" (*malak* YHWH). Selvaggio writes that a scholarly consensus exists that "the angel of the Lord" is a visible appearance of God. However, he says that though some believe this to be the preincarnate Son, this view is not "exegetically settled."[2]

Selvaggio does not explain what he means by the phrase "exegetically settled," but most likely it refers to something that has obtained scholarly consensus. Therefore, why do some (perhaps most) reject the concept of the preincarnate Son concerning this theophany? Is it because they think there could not be a revelation of the Trinity or even the idea of the multi-personality of the divine Being during this epoch of history?

2. Selvaggio, *Bondage to Liberty*, 32.

Such an assumption would bring us back to the problem of the dominance of history and culture in the hermeneutical process of interpreting Holy Scripture. Are we compelled to believe there could not be an early manifestation of the preincarnate Son? However, Luke says that to Cleopas and his companion, the risen Christ interpreted the scriptures, starting with Moses, as testifying of him. (Luke 24:27).

Exegetical markers in the title *angel of the* L*ORD* require understanding the Godhead's multipersonality. In their lexicon, Brown, Driver, and Briggs list as the first and primary definition of *malak* as a messenger who is sent.[3] Therefore, if Moses is confronted by a *malak* who is divine, who sent this messenger? It must also be someone divine. We are not dealing with an ancient polytheism, for this same Moses declares in the great Shema, "Hear, O Israel, the LORD our God, the LORD is One!" (Deut 6:4 NASB). Given these considerations, what other conclusion could we reach than there is more than one personal subsistence in the one divine essence?

The initiative of the Lord in establishing the Mosaic religion tells us at least two things. The first is that God is *central* to this religion, and the second is that it is Christocentric.

One unmistakably clear characteristic of the Mosaic religion is the emphasis on blood sacrifice. The Passover lamb with its blood displayed on the doorpost—the substitute for Israel's firstborn—begins this emphasis (Exod 12:3). The substitution was necessary because God promised that every firstborn son in Egypt would die. This necessity was because the Lord determined that he would send the angel of death throughout Egypt. Without the sacrifice of the lamb, the firstborn of the Hebrew slaves would suffer the same fate (Exod 12:12–13).

As we view the death of the firstborn (the tenth and last plague sent against Egypt), there is a distinction between this plague and the other nine. The people of Israel escaped the onerous effects of the plagues without anything required of them. Conversely, they are also the targets of the tenth plague, except for the sacrificial lamb. Why was there this difference in the last plague? The text does not inform the reader. Nonetheless, God declares that he would deliver the people from bondage in this final plague, even though Israel was not entirely innocent. (Were their hands spotless concerning the issues that rendered the death of Egyptian children?)

The Passover's appointment in what became the first month (see Exod 12:2) underscores its critical significance. How do we explain such

3. Brown et al., s.v. דְאָלַמ.

prominence assigned to it before giving the law? Does this not show that God's grace in redemption comes before the obedience to follow?

The emphasis of the Mosaic religion on blood sacrifice did not stop with the Passover. The institution of much of the sacrificial system had to do with blood sacrifice. However, it would take more space than we have at our disposal to detail each kind of sacrifice and its possible relationship with substitution. One says *possible relationship* because there were elements of the system that had no apparent connection with blood atonement. The grain offering and the thank offering are two that come readily to mind.

Nevertheless, there was one sacrifice where the concept of substitutionary atonement is unmistakable. This sacrifice was the Day of Atonement, Yom Kippur (as described in Lev 23:26–32). That day was considered the most solemn day of the religious calendar. The high priest confessed the people's sins over the heads of two goats. The one which was called the scapegoat was driven out into the wilderness, symbolizing the removal of sin from the people. The other goat they slaughtered, and the high priest took its blood into the holy of holies and presented it before the presence of God.

Two related but separate ideas were symbolized in the two goats. In bearing the people's sin away, the scapegoat displayed the concept called *expiation*, the taking away of sin. Because the high priest presented the blood of the second goat before God as a sacrifice for sin, the rite symbolized *propitiation*, the appeasement of the wrath of God against sin through the death of a substitute, in two ways. These ways were: (1) the necessity that God should remove sin, and (2) that God's displeasure against sin must be removed from the sinner by shedding blood.

There is another concept in Yom Kippur that was not present in the other sacrifices of the ceremonial law. This is the idea that the death of one victim can atone for the sins of many. Every family—or at most two small families together—had a lamb to sacrifice at Passover, since the blood was appointed to cover only those within that household. In many other sacrifices, individuals had to bring their own sacrifices. The concept of the one for the many was necessary for the transition from the shadow of the law to its fulfillment in Jesus Christ.

One aspect of Mosaic religion begs for attention: the centrality of *love* in it. Earlier, we mentioned the Shema (Israel's confession of faith) in Deut 6:4. The very next verse contains what is known as the greatest commandment: "You shall love the Lord your God with all your heart and with all your soul and with all your might" (NASB). Moreover, love for God does not end the matter, but love for one's neighbor is also commanded. One should not minimize the emphasis on love; Jesus said that upon those two commandments hang the whole of the Law and the Prophets (Matt 22:40).

Faith was as much a part of the Mosaic as the patriarchal religion, which is displayed positively and negatively. Hebrews tells us that Moses's renunciation of his favored position in the family of Pharaoh was an act of faith (Heb 11:24–27). Furthermore, his return to Egypt to confront the Egyptian monarch with God's command to release the Hebrew slaves undoubtedly illustrates his faith in God's promised deliverance.

Nonetheless, the importance of faith is seen negatively in its absence on the part of the first generation of Israelites that left Egypt. Their faithlessness led to manifold judgments leading to the ultimate curse of God upon that generation, "They shall not enter my rest" (4:3 NASB).

One scarcely needs to say that the Mosaic religion has a sizeable ethical element. God gave the Ten Commandments to Moses on Mt. Sinai, and YHWH wrote them upon tablets of stone. And he commanded Moses to put them in the ark of the covenant in the holy of holies, which was the focal point of Israel's religious life. There the presence of God was enthroned above the golden cherubim placed on the mercy seat. Thus, it was as if YHWH presided over the faith of Israel, enthroned upon the testimony of his moral law (see Exod 25:10–22).

However, this picture provides a hint of something more than religious ethics. Why was the depository of the Commandments surmounted by the *mercy seat*? The high priest entered once a year with the blood of the sacrifice that he sprinkled upon the mercy seat (Lev 16). This was God's grace interposing between the offended law and the execution of justice. This factor is, without doubt, a sign of what was to come.

The Mosaic religion continued with Joshua and the entrance of the people into the land of promise. Overall, there were few changes in religion during this time. However, there are some essential elements that I need to mention.

One of these elements is a view of the holiness of God. This view is evident from the time of Moses's call through the exodus and wilderness wanderings. However, it is appropriate to mention holiness at the point of the transfer of leadership from Moses to Joshua. Moses was not permitted to enter Canaan because he struck the rock for water rather than speaking to it as commanded. In this action, the Lord declared that Moses had not regarded him as holy (see Num 20:11–12).

Two other incidents in this transitional period also illustrate the holiness of God. The first is found in the crossing of the Jordan in which God commanded that the people stay two thousand cubits distant from the ark of the covenant (Josh 3:4). Only the holiness of the presence of the Lord can explain the need for over one-half mile separating the ark from the people. The second event is recorded in Josh 5:13–15 when the captain of the host of the Lord confronts Joshua. This confrontation was a divine encounter: Joshua was commanded to remove his shoes because he stood on holy ground. The encounter emphasized the holiness of the One who was to be worshiped.

There is one more aspect of the Mosaic religion that Scripture emphasizes in the time of Joshua as well as Moses. Israel's faith was both corporate and individual. Under Joshua, there is a mass circumcision of all the males of Israel born during the forty years in the wilderness (Josh 5). This event is a renewal of the covenant and is corporate. The individual aspect appears in Josh 24:15: "But if it is disagreeable in your sight to serve the Lord, choose for yourselves today whom you will serve: whether the gods which your fathers served, which were beyond the Euphrates River or the gods of the Amorites in whose land you are living; but as for me and my house, we will serve the Lord" (NASB). Both corporate and individual aspects are present in the events surrounding the sins of Achan. A judgment falls upon all Israel when Ai defeats them, but Achan was punished explicitly for his sin (Josh 7).

The Religion of Ancient Israel in the Period of the Judges

The time of the judges was a time of spiritual decline in Israel. Periods of short repentance punctuated this decline, but the spiral was ever downward. We do not look to this period to find examples of the true religion that God established among his people. Instead, we find either corruption of true religion or its abandonment by wholesale apostasy as the Israelites turned to the paganism of their neighbors.

Dr. Robert Godfrey suggests that the book of Judges was a polemic dating from the time of David and Solomon, stressing the necessity of the kingdom's coming. The twice repeated statement apparently confirms

Godfrey's judgment: "There was no king in Israel; everyone did what was right in his own eyes" (Judg 17:6; 21:25 ESV). This statement appears in the middle and at the end of Judges.

Nevertheless, one must guard against the supposition that the book of Judges is merely a human advocate's political justification of the monarchy. In the quoted words, the Holy Spirit is giving his analysis of the spiritual condition of the time, and we must take it to heart. It leads us to consider the divine paradox that points to Jesus Christ.

When Samuel is reluctant to heed the wishes of the people to "give us a king," the Lord comforts him with the knowledge that it was not Samuel that the people rejected but himself (1 Sam 8:6–7). YHWH was their king, but YHWH directed Samuel to consent to the demand and give the people a king after warning them what the result would be. After the false start with Saul, God chose David and established his house *forever*. In the fullness of time, Jesus is sent, "born of the seed of David according to the flesh; who was declared to be Son of God in power according to the Spirit of holiness by the resurrection of the dead" (Rom 1:3–4). Thus, the rejection of God as king, according to his mysterious providence, leads at last to the coming of a king who is God in the flesh.

From the perspective of human obedience, there is very little positive to say about Israel's religion during the time of the judges. However, from the divine perspective, there is a positive emphasis. This reminds us that Israel's continued existence is based upon divine forbearance and grace.

In Deut 28:15–68, Moses warned the Israelites regarding the consequences of disobedience to God's commands. We would expect that their turning away from the Lord would bring the wholesale destruction of the nation or their expulsion from the land of promise. Nevertheless, despite God's numerous judgments seen in Judges, there are just as many deliverances through the various saviors he sends. God allowed these men and women to deliver Israel from the devastating situations in which they found themselves. He tempered judgment with mercy.

In addition to witnessing God's grace that effected immediate deliverance, there was also the pointer to the One who was to come: Jesus Christ, the quintessential Savior and Deliverer. Without the expected fulfillment of his coming, there would have been no typological saviors to come to Israel's aid.

When we speak of the forbearing grace of God experienced by Israel, there is an emphasis upon a component of religious consciousness that should have made itself evident but often did not. This component is the necessary element of humility. Judgment mitigated, deferred, or delayed calls for humility and thanksgiving—these components, when present, emphasize forbearance and grace in one manner. When absent, patience and grace are emphasized in another fashion. The kindness of God, when extended to the ungrateful and proud, makes his grace shine even more brightly. Though we must add the caveat of Paul: "Are we to continue in sin so that grace may increase? May it never be!" (Rom 6:1–2 NASB).

There is one other matter that we ought to mention: that deliverance can come through the death of a savior. This concept one finds in the account of Samson. Though Samson was arguably the most flawed of the judges, he destroyed three thousand of Israel's oppressors in his death (Judg 16:23–30). We can justifiably say that this concept typologically points to Jesus Christ and the infinitely greater deliverance found in his death. In choosing the most flawed of the judges to bring a rescue of this kind, one could conceivably suggest that the Holy Spirit is pointing to Jesus as the sin-bearer, sinless though he is.

The Scriptures do not furnish data on whether any in Israel understood this concept in the death of Samson. Nevertheless, the typological significance was there and embedded in the words of the text, "So the dead that he killed at his death were more than the dead that he killed in his life" (Judg 16:30b).

The Religion of Israel in the Period of the Monarchy

As mentioned, the time of the judges was one of spiritual and religious decline. However, it would be a mistake to say of the monarchy that it was a time of uninterrupted spiritual and religious advancement. The spiritual and religious fortunes of Israel (and later Israel and Judah) tended to parallel the political life of the people. Even in the beginning, King Saul failed to understand the true inward spiritual nature of YHWH's religion. He was so deficient in this area that it led to the Lord's rejection of his dynasty (1 Sam 15:1–28). There was a brief golden age of religious faithfulness in the reign of David and the early years of Solomon. After that, religious devotion was spotty at best, and by the time of Jerusalem's final fall to Babylon, Ezekiel proclaimed that the spiritual state of the people of Judah made Sodom look righteous by comparison (16:46, 47).

Nevertheless, there were glimmers of real faithfulness even in the darkest times. For example, the Lord told Elijah, when he was in despair, "Yet I will leave 7,000 in Israel, all the knees that have not bowed to Baal and every mouth that has not kissed him" (1 Kgs 19:18 NASB). Furthermore, unlike in the period of the judges, we do not have to gather what true religion was by inverting the false. Positive examples of Israel's religion give us data for the inquiry.

Regarding the period of the monarchy, whether united or divided, the problem we face in studying its religion is the sheer amount of information. The Old Testament portion written during this time is obviously the largest. It includes most of the material in Samuel through Chronicles, all the wisdom literature (except for Job), most of the psalms, and many written prophets.

We spoke previously of the emphasis on love for God in the Mosaic period, as revealed in Deut 6:5–6. We might ask, "What is the outward manifestation of love to God?" Would it not be praise? Praise, in the form of singing, is most noticeably evident in the Psalter, and almost the entire Psalter comes from the monarchy period.

If our interest was a study of the form of Israel's religion, one could survey the types of psalms, the nature of their poetic structure, and how they were employed in Israel's worship. However, our interest is in the essence of the Lord's religion instituted among his Old Testament saints. For our purposes, the theology of the psalms is of greater interest.

The praise of God in songs did not begin with the monarchy. There is biblical evidence of this in previous eras (e.g., the Song of Moses and the Song of Deborah). We would make an unwarranted assumption if we suggested that the relative infrequency of recorded praise songs in the previous epoch signified that not much singing took place. The limited genres of canonical literature from those epochs do not make the record of songs of praise very likely. Conversely, the literature from the monarchical period is more amenable to recording such songs.

Sincere singing in praise is one of the manifestations of love for God. As already noted, this love was one of the essential elements of Israel's religion in the era of Moses and Joshua. Thus, the prominence of singing praise in David's reign witnesses the love of God present at that time in the faithful in Israel.

Several elements of this period are of great significance in perceiving the unity of Old Testament and New Testament religion. The concepts of the promised Messiah, the atonement, and the resurrection are chief among these elements.

Nevertheless, the prevalence of a hermeneutic that allows the dominance of history and culture to drive it gives us trouble at this point. The orthodox scholars that utilize this method believe that we can look back upon this epoch and see the unity of the Testaments in hindsight, but they seem to loathe the idea that the inspired writers were aware that their pens were speaking of matters beyond their age. Nonetheless, it is curious that there is not the same reticence concerning the coming of "the great and terrible day of the Lord" (Mal 4:5 NASB). This event was prophesied as a cataclysm of world-shaking proportions bringing an end to all God's enemies through his judgment. Why were the Old Testament pre-exilic prophets able to speak *with understanding* of a final judgment when we are told they could not write *with an understanding* of the Messiah, his atonement, and the resurrection?

Why was the final judgment considered relevant to the Old Testament prophets, yet the Messiah and his work were not? The first matter is further in the future than the others. We evidently must ask permission to treat the revelation of the Messiah and his work as much a conscious part of Israel's religion as readily as the revelation of God's final judgment.

Another concept known as prophetic foreshortening suggests that the prophetic view of the Messiah and his advent combined his first and second comings as if they were one event. Nevertheless, this is a far cry from the idea that God's final judgment upon the sin-cursed world had no connection to the Messiah of which the prophets were aware.

We should proceed here on the assumption that the prophets and other inspired writers of this period *knew* that they were writing of him and the doctrines pertaining to his person and work. If this seems to beg the question by assuming that they had such knowledge, we need only reply that thinking that texts that appear to speak of the Messiah only by hindsight *also* beg the question. For example, in Ps 2:7 we read, "He said to Me, 'You are My Son, today I have begotten You'" (NASB). The suggestion that David was speaking of himself is from an assumption that his historical era made it impossible for him to give a direct prophecy concerning his Savior.

Let us be perfectly straightforward. If the Old Testament witness at this time to the Messiah, his person, and his work was but a second reading of the texts, then there was *no* continuity between the religion of ancient Israel and our own. Upon what was salvation based? Upon whom did the

Israelites place their hope of sins forgiven? On what basis, for example, did David plea for that forgiveness when he confessed that he had no sacrifice he could offer to God in atonement for his sin? There are no answers to these questions if Jesus Christ, his death, and resurrection are ruled out of court at the outset. What was the place of faith during the monarchy? If there was no object of faith, then faith in that period ceased to be an *instrument* of justification. Instead, it became the *means* of justification since it had no justifying object upon which to rest. If the answer was that God, unipersonal and preincarnate, was the justifying object of faith, then how could they answer the question of how God could justify sinners while still being just? How could the psalmist say, "but there is forgiveness with You that You may be feared" (Ps 130:4 NASB)? Upon what was his confidence based?

The standard answer to these questions is that the faith that justified the saints of this and previous eras was faith in God's promise *as they understood it*. God promised that he would somehow redeem Israel from her sins and enemies. Is this enough? Is sufficient revelation given in an ambiguous promise that the saints might know the purpose of their belief?

Adam and Eve believed God would provide the woman's seed to crush the serpent's head (Gen 3:15, 20). Abraham believed that through the promised seed, all the families of the world would bless themselves (Gen 22:18). Is this amorphous *somehow* an advance upon the former promises? Is it not instead a regression? How could these people understand that God must be just and the justifier of believers? Was not a concept of Messiah necessary to them as well as the companion concept that he would be the One to whom the sacrifices of the law pointed? Did they actually believe that the blood of bulls and goats could take away sin? To their minds, were the Messiah and sacrifice two hermetically sealed concepts?

These questions should not be a matter of doubt. Suppose merely general promises, adherence to a sacrificial system that pointed no further than itself, and sincere but imperfect obedience to God's law was enough to save the saints of the monarchy. Why should justification be limited to faith in Jesus *only* from the New Testament onward? If Old Testament saints could be justified outside of Jesus Christ, why can't we?

Some of the sacred writings from the monarchy period seem to cry out about a particular coming One who is the hope of redemption for the people of God. In those writings, if we believe that the inspired writer had no intention to speak of Christ, he is at a loss to know of whom he intended to speak.

Isaiah 53:6 is a case in point: "All of us, like sheep, have gone astray, each of us has turned to his own way; but the Lord has caused the iniquity of us all to fall on Him" (NASB). Suppose the prophet's original intention in these words had nothing to do with a personal and individual redeemer and sin-bearer. In that case, we must follow the interpretation of the unbelieving rabbis, who identify the servant as Israel personified.

Such an interpretation makes a hash of the prophet's words. Does he intend to say, "*All of us* (the whole number of Israel individually considered), like sheep, have gone astray, each of us has turned to his own way; *but* (conjunction of contrast) the Lord has caused the wrongdoing *of us all* (see above) to fall on *him* (Israel collectively considered and personified)?" In such an interpretation, the distinction between *all of us* or *us all* and *him* is a distinction without a difference. The statement becomes a mere tautology; Israel is guilty of Israel's sins. The entire chapter becomes unintelligible without the intentional inclusion in Isa 53 of the Messiah, his atonement, and resurrection.

Neither is this a singular instance of messianic prophecy. Isaiah 9:6–7 is another prophecy that is unintelligible if it must be confined to the historical epoch and culture of Isaiah's time. It reads,

> For a [C]hild will be born to us, a [S]on will be given to us;
> And the government will rest on His shoulders;
> And His name will be called
> Wonderful Counselor, Mighty God, Eternal Father, Prince of Peace.
> There will be no end to the increase of His government or of peace
> On the throne of David and over his kingdom,
> To establish it and to uphold it with justice and righteousness
> From then on and forevermore.
> The zeal of the Lord of armies will accomplish this. (NASB)

Who is this Child? If Isaiah intended to speak of a descendant of David of his own historical and cultural period, he engaged in hyperbole of truly infinite proportions. Each of the four titles of the child fairly drips with deity, and they are titles that no man other than our Lord Jesus Christ deserves to assume. If Isaiah intended a merely human individual, how does one acquit him of blasphemy?

Few believing scholars deny that Isaiah intended to speak of the Messiah. Nonetheless, instead of acknowledging exceptions to their rules in these passages, why do they not recognize the texts as proof against their false and dangerous principles of interpretation?

What is true in the Isaiah passages is also true in many of the messianic psalms. Nevertheless, many contemporary interpreters categorize them first and immediately as enthronement psalms utilizing admitted hyperbole[4] and only secondarily as pointing beyond the human king.

This practice is why I have endeavored to show that such a hermeneutic places grave doubts upon the nature and content of the religion at the time and upon the validity of the once *and for all* atonement of Jesus Christ. If the people of David's day needed no Messiah, why does anyone?

Consider these words from Ps 2:10–12: "Now therefore, O kings, show discernment; take warning, O judges of the earth. Worship the Lord with reverence and rejoice with trembling. Do homage to the Son, that He not become angry, and you perish in the way, for His wrath may soon be kindled. How blessed are all who take refuge in Him!" (NASB). These are words that place *the Lord* and *the Son* on a plane of equality. They also encourage a personal relationship with *the Son* as a means of avoiding destruction, and extol taking refuge in him as a way of blessedness. Did anyone's eternal destiny depend upon a relationship with David equal to that of God? Conversely, is it not apparent that David points to the unique Son that God would send as this source of eternal safety and blessedness?

The Exilic and Post-Exilic Religion of Israel

God's revelation addressed to his people at the time of the exile parallels the revelation addressed to them in the latter stages of the monarchies. Indeed, we would be justified in saying that the edges are somewhat blurred. For example, though scholars consider Ezekiel an exilic prophet, much of his prophecy is directed at those still living in Jerusalem in the last days of the monarchy. Yet, when we compare Ezekiel to Jeremiah—a pre-exilic prophet—we find that their ministries overlap, and the message that they declare is also very similar.

4. Some make the hazardous suggestion that in using hyperbole, the psalmists merely followed the example of the surrounding nations that viewed their rulers as semi-divine beings. Why should God, who strenuously condemns the false worship of the nations, allow his instruments of revelation to follow the heathen nations in this regard?

Nevertheless, outwardly there was a remarkable transformation in Israel's religion during the exile. The temple of Solomon was destroyed in Babylon's final conquest of Judah and Jerusalem. In addition, before this destruction, the glory of YHWH departed from the temple as Ezekiel saw in his vision (10:18).

This outward change paralleled an inward change on the part of many of the exiles. Humility replaced pride. An example of this change appears in Ps 137:1–4:

> By the rivers of Babylon, there we sat down, yes we wept, when
> we remembered Zion. Upon the willows in the middle thereof,
> we hung up our harps.
> For, there, those who carried us away captive asked of us a song,
> And those that plundered us *requested* mirth, *saying*,
> "Sing for us one of the songs of Zion."
> How shall we sing YHWH's song in a foreign land?

Representatives of this change of heart appear in Nehemiah, Ezra, Zerubbabel, and others. It seemed that Israel had learned their lesson about the abominable character of idolatry.

However, the spiritual state in the exile is not entirely positive, and the rebuke that God gives to the elders of Israel in Ezekiel is powerful. The opening of chapter 14 of his prophecy is an example:

> Then some elders of Israel came to me and sat down before me. And the word of the Lord came to me, saying, "Son of man, these men have set up their idols in their hearts and have put in front of their faces the stumbling block of their wrongdoing. Should I let Myself be consulted by them at all? Therefore speak to them and tell them, 'This is what the Lord God says: "Anyone of the house of Israel who sets up his idols in his heart, puts in front of his face the stumbling block of his wrongdoing, and then comes to the prophet, I the Lord will let Myself answer him in the matter in view of the multitude of his idols, in order to take hold of the hearts of the house of Israel who have turned away from Me due to all their idols."'"(Ezek 14:1–5 NASB)

We note in the text the phrase "set up idols in their hearts." This phrase has an ominous ring to it both in terms of the people of the exile and those of the post-exilic period. The end of outward idolatry among the Jews returning to the land and those living in the diaspora did not bring in the golden age of pure religion. The rebukes delivered to Israel by post-exilic prophets attest to this fact, as does the four hundred years of divine silence before the appearance of the Messiah and his forerunner.

The Old Testament does not describe the rise of the formalistic and hypocritical ritualism of the priestly party (Sadducees) or the rise of the legalistic and hypocritical ritualism of the scribes and Pharisees. However, they did develop because they were in full flower in the first century. John the Baptist saw the nation's spiritual state as a dead tree that needed cutting down, or a threshing floor that needed winnowing (Luke 3:7–9).

In Malachi, the hope of the Messiah was centered in the picture of the refining and purifying of Israel. However, instead of the cleansing of hearts and consciences, it had been transformed by the Jews into the hope of a nationalistic hero who would defeat Israel's foes and bring in a golden age founded upon the Messiah's external victories. Malachi's question, "But who can endure the day of His coming?" (Mal 3:2 NASB) was treated in the time of Jesus as a question for the gentiles, not for Israel.

Malachi and his messianic hope reflected the nature of the pure religion in ancient Israel. On the other hand, the Pharisees and Sadducees were the true descendants of the adulterous generation that incurred prophetic denunciation and rebuke.

Conclusion

These chapters are meant to show that, *in essence*, the religion of the church in the Old Testament is the same as the religion of the church in the New Testament. Differences are based on the historical position regarding the cross. The concept of the suffering savior was known as far back as Gen 3:15. Likewise, Ps 22 reveals details of the crucifixion—namely, the division of the garments—and Isa 53 gives more. Other specific details were not yet known. However, there is enough scriptural material to point believers to the Messiah and his saving work in the Old Testament as well as in the New.

The Old Testament prophetic forth-telling in judgment upon individual and corporate sin is parallel in the Bible to Jesus's and his apostles' denunciation of sin as their pleas for gospel obedience. Yet, the presence of an ethical emphasis in either Testament is not unique among religions and could lead one astray from the essential character of biblical faith. Instead, biblical faith looks to God's free and unmerited favor and what he has done for us and in us through Christ, the Messiah.

10

The Unity of Scripture and Postmodernism

Introduction

A thoughtful reader may think, "What's all the fuss?" Isn't the question concerning the unity of God's word an academic issue better left to the scholars than to trouble the consciousness of the average believer? This reader may suggest that the thesis propounded is dangerous, threatening to make Scripture ahistorical and thus irrelevant to those living in any historical or cultural framework. Nevertheless, the author *has* foreseen this reasoning from the outset.

The word of God is not ahistorical! The Holy Spirit, the ultimate Author of Holy Scripture, is trans-temporal and trans-cultural. He dwells in eternity, but his providence guides both history and culture. Nothing comes as a novelty to God; he knows history and culture's flux from eternity past.

The objections need to be confronted. We must stress the utter necessity of the unity of Scripture in this postmodern world. Our culture has gone from Pilate's question, "What is truth?" (John 18:38) to the positive denial of truth in any but the most relativistic sense. The postmodernist claims that my truth is *my* truth, and your truth is *yours*. In this movement into absolute relativism, the postmodernists have a problem. While claiming to go beyond Kant's *Critique of Pure Reason* by denying the existence of a reality beyond the senses, postmodernists find themselves warring against the idea that perception of the senses should, in any manner, hold them prisoner. On the one hand, they deny the existence of a world outside themselves where abstract concepts such as truth exist. On the other hand, those who have followed their teaching attempt to escape the reality that their senses present to them if it is uncongenial to their wishes at all.

The concept of gender fluidity is an example. The postmodernists deny the perception of human anatomy concerning gender as relevant to gender identity. They believe the personal conviction of one's gender identity is the supreme judge of its *truth*. However, this is just the choice of one set of perceptions instead of the other. One is outward and physical, the other inward and psychological; who is to choose?

This question brings us full circle to the skepticism of Pilate and his question "What is truth?" expressed when Jesus stood before him at his trial. Jesus responded that he had a duty to bear witness to the truth. However, in the way Pilate asks the question, he denies that there is any such thing.

Pilate had reason to want skepticism to prevail. He was part of the corrupt system of the Roman government that dispensed justice based upon the bribery of the highest bidder. There is nothing blameworthy in the practice if there is no such thing as truth. In that case, *justice* is just a word, and a judge does not administer it; instead, he creates it. There is no truth to vindicate but only a decision to render on whatever grounds one wishes.

Pilate's escape from the truth can be seen in the hypocritical washing of his hands after he had delivered Jesus to be crucified. The facts screamed that it was his responsibility—Jesus was tortured and crucified by Roman soldiers manifestly under Pilate's orders. The symbolic performance of handwashing did nothing to change the reality of the situation; Jesus was cruelly scourged and crucified under the commands of Pilate (Matt 27:24–26).

Postmodernism finds itself in Pilate's camp. Yet, if such a thing as truth exists, there is a standard by which our actions may be judged. In that case, conscience is a witness to guilt as a reality. It is not a remnant of previous religious epochs of our history. Jesus had already answered Pilate's question in his high priestly prayer: "Sanctify them in truth; *Your word is truth*" (John 17:17 NASB, emphasis mine).

However, this chapter will not give a critique of postmodernism and all its ramifications. Instead, it will analyze the lost ideas of Scripture's unity and relevance, playing into the hands of postmodern notions of truth.

Did the view of the Bible as a diverse collection of writings, each bound to its historical and cultural settings, play a part in the loss of regard for the Bible as the source of absolute truth and standard of ethical norms? I am convinced that it did.

The Reality of Truth

In 1855 James Henley Thornwell published a book taken from a series of discourses he had given at the College of South Carolina in 1851 when he was president and chaplain of that institution. The addresses were about the subject of *truth*. Dr. Thornwell did not use any of these discourses to prove the reality of truth. He assumed that all his readers knew that there was such a thing. Thornwell was interested in pressing upon his readers the duties that stem from truth's existence. These are the need to love and practice the truth.

Yet, in less than twenty years after this book's publication, German rationalism and its attack upon the inspiration and authority of Holy Scripture would make significant inroads in America's religious life. Nevertheless, even then, there was a consensus that truth existed, in whatever way one might debate the source and standard of truth.

Truth is real. The skepticism that denies this does not stand up to the scrutiny of experience. The parents tell the toddler that he or she must not touch the hot stove. Surely, Momma and Poppa do not know what they are talking about, so the stove is touched, and the truth of the parents' words is displayed. A thief points a firearm at someone's head. He might reason this is only his perception of a gun; there may be nothing there. The thief pulls the trigger, the gun discharges, and the victim suffers a fatal wound.

Skeptics like David Hume may tell me that these comments are based upon merely the past observance of the twists of fate, and they have nothing to do with future events since there is no such thing as causality. Nevertheless, let one human being live life entirely as a skeptic, basing actions on no past events, and let another live life learning from experience. Let us see which person lives the longest.

I have been speaking of the concept of the connection between perception and reality. Almost all human beings acknowledge the *practical* use of this kind of truth. Are the arguments above, therefore, deceptive? Not at all. The practical living done by those who deny the truth in its ultimate form is the living done upon borrowed capital. It might be better to call it stolen capital; there is an acknowledged relationship between lender and borrower. The denier of ultimate truth recognizes no such association. In a universe of pure randomness without causation, there ought not to be a way of practical truth. Yet multitudes live upon the stolen capital of a system founded upon truth.

One speaks of the *laws of chance* and can make charts of predicted future outcomes. Nevertheless, this is a misuse of the word *chance*. If we use a synonym, *chaos*, and interchange it in the phrase, we immediately see the absurdity of such a thing. *The laws of chaos*, what an idea! The word *chance* in the expression must mean something different, which appears in the alternate phrase, *the laws of probability*. Probability and chance are two very different matters.

The fact of such things as the laws of probability confronts us with the force that drives such laws. To say that this is the *natural* result of randomness is to make an assertion that supplies no reason for its being so. Suppose we cannot determine the specific effects of a random event. Why can a general pattern of the outcome of ten thousand random events be accurately predicted? If randomness forbids knowing which side of a flipped coin will land, how is it possible to know that the coin will not land on the same side when flipped a hundred times, a thousand times, ten thousand times, or an infinite number of times?

The usual answer is that the laws of probability do not forbid the possibility of such occurrences but render them exceedingly small. Yet surely no one would grant the slightest possibility of the suggestion of an infinite number of times. In Tom Stoppard's play *Rosencrantz and Guildenstern Are Dead*, which begins in the middle of a coin-flipping contest that has the coin come up heads eighty-five times, the playwright in the stage directions says, "The run of *heads* is impossible." One might quibble at the absolute interpretation of the word *impossible*. Still, if Stoppard's audience deemed the event that he dramatizes as possible, it would lose all its dramatic effect as the play's opening.[1]

The fact is that the tossing of coins is not the product of chaos or laws that have behind them no divine sanction, and they are the demonstration of divine providence. "The lot is cast into the lap, but its every decision is from the Lord" (Prov 16:33 NASB). A chaotic world is one in which truth does not exist because truth and meaning are inseparable. Therefore, the denial of truth is a denial of purpose, and it is a denial of every

1. Stoppard, *Rosencrantz and Guildenstern*, 1–7. Stoppard's play is meant to exhibit the meaningless state of existence, but to do this, he must cook the books, so to speak, and begin the play with a situation that he himself calls impossible.

purpose—even the alleged purpose of postmodernism's denial of truth. Conversely, the affirmation of truth, as found in the triune God, is an affirmation of meaning, even giving us the ability to analyze the faulty meaning of the denial of truth by postmodernism.

Truth and Meaning

The previous section brings us to a more significant expression of the relationship between truth and meaning. This relationship manifests itself in the antithesis to which the concept of truth gives rise. We could not know the truth if there were no falsehoods or errors with which to contrast it. In a world where falsehood and error were impossible, truth as a concept would pass unnoticed; it would be a given. I grant that all communication would correspond to reality, but saying that would be like saying, "All fish swim"—it would be a mere tautology.

Moreover, the truth or falsehood of anything depends upon the meaning conveyed by it. Without meaning, there is no tool to determine truth or falsity. Statements that are neither true nor false are simply meaningless, and questions you cannot answer with truth or falsehood are merely useless. How would we respond to the following question: "Is it farther to New York or by bus?" To give another example, how would we answer, "How many ducks in a gallon?"

The letters *khfdbceryjfdghjgrkl* strung together have no meaning. The blind pressing of one finger on the keyboard created them, but they would still have no sense even if the process had produced an English word. And even if a typewriting monkey given enough time could produce the form of every book in the British Museum, in all its millions of pages, there would still be no meaning, for they would convey nothing from the monkeys' minds to the reader's mind.

In a universe of chaos that possessed no truth, there would be no possibility of meaningful communication between persons. Any apparent meaning would be only *apparent* with no actual existence.

Some will say there *is* meaning even without truth. The objectors will say they always carry on conversations, and both parties can derive some meaning. However, how does either party know whether the words said have the same meaning for each other? What if the conversation's meaningfulness depends solely on the parties forcing the terms to mesh with their own? If one party goes away and finds that the information he sought seemed to *work*, how do they know that wasn't just a fortuitous event? In an entirely chaotic world, no word is guaranteed to have the slightest meaning.

People can *deny* the truth and still find meaning in their daily lives, but denial does not annihilate truth. They simply live on the borrowed capital of the truth that they deny, and stand upon a platform, the existence of which they refuse to acknowledge!

Truth and Time

If at least practical truth (as distinct from absolute truth) is granted, will it also be granted that some sort of truth is universal? Does it exist for any time, in any place, under any circumstances, and for any person? The postmodern answer to this question appears to be no. Even the kind of truth granted to exist is only valid for one age or epoch in its minimal manner. For example, the *truths* accepted in the modern world are no longer valid in the postmodern world.

At this point, we must distinguish between singulars and plurals. The Christian grants that some truths (plural) are subject to the changing circumstances of the time. In addition, we staunchly maintain that there is timeless Truth (singular).

For example, as I sit at my desk typing, the statement is true that I am in my residence. When the reader reads those words, the report may not be accurate. Nonetheless, it is always true that I am either in my residence or *not* in my residence. In logic, this is the law of the excluded middle.

The universality of Truth does not begin and end with the tautological (i.e., a statement that cannot be false, e.g., red is red). It extends further. "You shall not murder" is regarded by Christians as a universal prohibition. The prosecutions of its violators stretch from Cain, the first man to be born of a woman, to the sentences meted out to criminals today. The moral law that the Lord implanted in the hearts of Adam and Eve God still places within the hearts of every rational human being.

Postmodernism denies this truth partly because postmodernism confuses *manners* with *morals*. Therefore, concerning the question of origin, it seems there is no difference between a law forbidding homicide today and the taboo of the ancient Philistines concerning not treading upon the threshold of their god Dagon. Both, to the postmodern mind, are the product of human institutions. The prohibition of murder still exists because each succeeding generation has validated it; the ancient taboo is moribund because succeeding generations have found it useless. Of course, if succeeding generations find punishing homicide equally useless to them, it, too, might rightly become passé.

Nevertheless, *morals* and *manners* are different things. Manners are human institutions, but true morality is the institution of the immutable and eternal God. Winston Churchill is famously credited with parodying a grammatical convention with the statement, "Ending a sentence with a preposition is something up with which I will not put." He could do so without incurring any moral guilt. However, those that murder their neighbor, though human justice may never touch them, have taken upon themselves the blame that will bring them to God's judgment seat.

Moses stood on Mt. Sinai over three thousand years ago. The Ten Commandments are still in effect because the finger of God wrote them on the tablets of stone. God has not changed, and his will for his creatures has not changed.

Nor is it only moral truth that is timeless. The truth founded upon nature that God created is timeless; God alone may overrule it at his pleasure. Earth's movement on its axis, and its circuit around the sun, remain while it exists. The Creator can interfere with these things, but no one else. The Scriptures testify to the permanency of these things until the consummation.

We have not yet exhausted the catalog of timeless truth. Those truths describing the triune God's person and work are also timeless. "Believe in the Lord Jesus, and you will be saved, you and your household" (Acts 16:31 NASB) is a statement that is not limited to the Philippian jailer. "God is love" (1 John 4:8 NASB) is also universally true.

This declaration is, in part, but only in part, what lies behind YHWH's statement to Moses: "I Am that I Am" (Exod 3:14 NASB). A belief in chaos refuses timeless truth because chaos is ever changing. The immutable God secures eternal verity because he is eternally immutable. From chaos, one can never reach the truth. The One who is Alpha and Omega guarantees that truth is both real and eternal.

Timeless Truth and the Unity of Scripture in Respect to Postmodernism

Bible believers point to the Scripture's teaching as the reason for opposing postmodern thought, and all that flows from it. With its dismissal of absolute truth, postmodernism dismisses the Bible as merely a relic of the past and a dangerous relic at that. It is a relic because it presents nothing more than the opinions of ancient people concerning religion. It is hazardous because the church has used it to impress these ancient ideas upon her followers. Postmodernism believes the Scriptures are an irrelevancy and their teachings outdated, outmoded, and outlandish.

Those who are orthodox Christians, believing in the inspiration and authority of Scripture, are rightly appalled by such an attitude. The insults hurt us, but we are equally saddened by the closure that such an attitude gives to any witness to postmodern humanity. The only secure authority upon which one can stand is that of the infallible word of God. What do we have to say if the Bible is ruled out of the public square?

We believe in timeless truth and are convinced that this truth is contained in the scriptures of the Old and New Testaments. We must never retreat from that position lest we lose our way in the sea of chaos with our postmodern opponents. The unity of Scripture is one of the truths we ought to hold with a grip of iron.

However, do we play into the postmodernists' hands when we treat the Scriptures as a diverse anthology of ancient writings whose interpretation finds no significance outside the historical epoch and culture of the time of the writing of each document? We may claim that the Bible's relevance to the contemporary world continues because God (the Holy Spirit) makes them relevant to us in a manner utterly absent from the original intention of the human writers of the text. This idea may satisfy some Christian scholars, but what will the postmodernist think of such arguments? Will he not see this as using a deus ex machina (i.e., God out of the box)? Will the postmodernist perceive this as a mechanism by which we solve inconvenient discrepancies by a sort of magic transposition with no historical roots in the text?

For example, what is the postmodern response to the explanation of Ps 2 that insists that David was speaking of himself and intended the words to have no other meaning? And that the Holy Spirit only intended for the generation beginning with the first century to see an application to the Lord Jesus Christ? Christians, who believe in the Holy Spirit, may be content with his authority for such use. However, would not the postmodernist question why the application cannot be to another person, even one who has not appeared yet on the world stage?

In the example I have just given, we can reply to the postmodernist that the apostolic witness of the New Testament does validate such an application. However, what of other texts not directly quoted in the New Testament as applying to Christ Jesus? Not every text from the Old Testament that has *application* to Jesus finds a quotation in the New Testament, and Isa 9:6–7 is a case in point. The prophet uses words that are no more grandiose than the words of Pss 2, 45, 72, or 110. How do we know that the Holy Spirit intends us to see Jesus Christ in these passages if the prophet did not? Conversely, if we firmly believe Isaiah *intended* the Messiah, how do we conclude such a thing, when we do not believe it in the case of the psalmists who use similar language?

Is it possible that the watching postmodern world, as it beholds the machinations of Christian scholars, will make comments such as, "See, they agree with us when they actually interpret the text!"; or "They tacitly admit that these are only ancient writings that have no relevancy to the postmodern world"; or "All the applications they try to make are nothing but smoke and mirrors."

The biblical scholar may be isolated from these criticisms in his ivory tower. Unbelievers, nevertheless, can read their commentaries. They can see the hesitancy of scholars to find Jesus Christ unambiguously and intentionally in the texts of the Old Testament. They can announce to the sheep they have seduced that the church is secretly on their side.

The controversy with which this work is concerned is not just a scholarly debate, it is a controversy that has *great* relevance to what is going on in our society. Men and women, young people, and children are being deluded and sucked into the chaos of postmodernism. Drug addiction, suicide, and unspeakable abominations abound. Could we be complicit because, wittingly or unwittingly, we have carved the Bible into hermetically sealed parts that have only an external relationship to one another? May God grant that this is not the case! Nevertheless, if this is so, may this brief volume be seen as a call to *ruthlessly* examine the consequences of our practices in biblical scholarship!

Appendix A

New Testament Traces of the Knowledge of the Person of the Holy Spirit in the Old Testament

Introduction

One view that has gained the consensus of contemporary biblical scholars is that the distinct persons of the Godhead were unknown in the Old Testament. One of the more extreme manifestations of this understanding appears in a compendium titled *Presence, Power and Promise: the Role of the Spirit of God in the Old Testament.*[1] The editors argue that the Holy Spirit as a person is not found in the Old Testament, not even in a veiled form. They explain that his presence in the sacred writings would tempt ancient Israel into polytheism. The Spirit of God, they maintain, was understood to be nothing more than the outpouring of God's power and divine influence. A less extreme view acknowledges *hints* about the plurality of persons in the divine essence in the Old Testament but no more than hints.

Many orthodox scholars hold a view that before the appearance of the incarnate Christ and the establishment of the New Testament church, there was no need for the people of God to know the doctrine of the Trinity. Why would this be the case? If the answer is that God needed to show a distinction between Jews and Christians (Israel and the church), then why did Paul bewail the unbelief of the Jews of the first century? According to Eph 2:11–22, the purpose of Christ and his sacrifice is to break down the "middle wall of partition" between Jews and gentiles—not build it higher.

1. Firth and Wegner, *Presence, Power and Promise.*

Correcting this view from the pages of the Old Testament requires labor far beyond the scope of this book. Nevertheless, there are hints in the New Testament that distinct persons of the Trinity were known previous to the first century. I want to show specifically that this general statement is true of the Holy Spirit as a *person*.

If the person of the Holy Spirit was unknown before the coming of our Lord, we might expect some form of introduction to his appearance before it occurs. Nevertheless, it is not the case that he receives such an introduction. He is mentioned by speakers in the Gospels and Acts as if the audience knows something of his identity.

Traces in the Gospels[2]

Luke 1:5–21 records Zechariah's vision in the temple, promising the birth of John the Baptist. In verse 15, the angel announces the filling of John with the Holy Spirit from his mother's womb. The language is precise—*Holy Spirit*—and this is distinct from how the angel refers to John's coming "in the spirit and power of Elijah" (Luke 1:17 NASB). Elijah's spirit is a part of himself, while the angel speaks of the Spirit of God as a person, and he expects Zechariah to know of whom he speaks. There is no explanation for the identity of the Spirit. We might ask why the angel (presumably Gabriel) should expect such knowledge on Zechariah's part if the Holy Spirit was previously unknown as a person. Zechariah has questions about the angelic announcement, and he receives chastisement for them. Nevertheless, he asks no questions about the person of the Spirit.

In the next section of Luke, we come to the annunciation in which Gabriel announces to Mary that she will give birth to the Son of God. In answer to her question about how she, a virgin, could give birth, the angel tells her that the Holy Spirit will come upon her and the power of the Most High will overshadow her. Again, Gabriel mentions the Spirit without further proof of his identity, and he is associated with "the power of the Most High" (Luke 1:35 NASB). Nevertheless, Gabriel doesn't speak as if he were hiding the Spirit's identity, but the angel speaks of him as known to Mary, a humble Nazarene maiden.

Matthew 1:18–21 records the heavenly vision Joseph received in a dream concerning Jesus's birth. The Gospel writer informs us that Mary

2. In the following discussion the phrase *the Holy Spirit* will be used with the assumption that it refers to his personality.

was "found to be with child by the Holy Spirit" (v. 18 NASB). Admittedly, Matthew wrote these words when the Holy Spirit was known as a person by the church. Nevertheless, the angel uses the same designation, "by the Holy Spirit," when he speaks to Joseph (v. 20). In addition, there is also no attempt to explain who the Holy Spirit is as if he was some previously unknown person. Why was this not necessary? The answer that seems most reasonable is that he was not previously unknown. Even a humble Nazarene carpenter knew something of who he was!

As we move forward, we come to the testimony of John the Baptist in the Gospel of Luke. There John proclaims that the One who is coming will baptize people "in the Holy Spirit" (Luke 3:16 NASB). The preposition used is significant. He says *in* the Holy Spirit, not *with* the Holy Spirit. The latter alternative suggests an impersonal power, but the former implies that the Holy Spirit is personal.

Jesus warns his apostles of their future persecution in Matt 10:16–20. He tells them not to worry about what they are to say in these words: "For it is not you who speak, but the Spirit of your Father speaking through you" (v. 20 ESV). Note that Jesus says that "the Spirit of your Father" speaks. This language isn't a reference to an impersonal power. If Jesus meant no more than God would speak for them, little reason existed to refer to the Spirit. He referred to a person connected to the Father, yet a person in his own right. Jesus expected them to know of whom he spoke. In the parallel passage in Luke 12:12, *the Holy Spirit* will give the apostles the words to say in the hour of persecution.

We come next to passages that I consider inexplicable without Jesus's expectation that his audience knew of whom he spoke. In Matt 12:28–32, Jesus warns against the unforgivable sin: blasphemy against the Holy Spirit. In this context, the Holy Spirit is described in three separate ways. First, he is called the "Spirit of God," then Jesus calls him simply "the Spirit," and finally, he is "the Holy Spirit." How we might ask, is it possible to blaspheme something that is merely an impersonal force? Jesus expects his hearers to recognize the One of whom he speaks. If they only understood Jesus as speaking of a unipersonal Being, how would they understand the other blasphemies that Jesus says will be forgiven? In that case, wherein lies the difference? Why is no such explanation given if the Holy Spirit as a separate person of the Godhead, was unknown to his audience? This question is pertinent primarily because of the distinction between blasphemies that will and will not receive forgiveness.

Mark's parallel passage distinguishes blasphemy against the Son of Man from blasphemy against the Holy Spirit. It will not do to say that Jesus's audience did not believe in the deity of the Son of Man, and Jesus did. Moreover, he expected them to understand his words. If they did not understand both the Son of Man's divinity and the Holy Spirit's distinct personality, then the opacity of Jesus's words is increased, not lessened.

In John 14:15–21, we find a passage that may seem to contradict my thesis that Israel had some knowledge of the Holy Spirit previous to the New Testament era. There Jesus says to his apostles, "I will ask the Father, and He will give you another Helper, that He may be with you forever; *that is* the Spirit of truth, whom the world cannot receive, because it does not see Him or know Him, *but* you know Him because He abides with you and will be in you" (vv. 16–17 NASB).

Some might ask how Jews of the first century knew the Holy Spirit if Jesus says the world does not know him. In response, Jesus's use of the word *world* is most likely not a reference to God's covenant people. The world at large does not have any knowledge of the person of the Holy Spirit, and this is to say nothing of the multipersonal nature of God. In addition, there is mention in the passage of all three persons of the Trinity. The Son will ask the Father for the gift of another Helper, and the Holy Spirit is the person given.

Walter Kaiser Jr. suggests that an alternate reading of the text gives reason to believe that the indwelling of the Spirit is a statement of a present reality, not a future occurrence (i.e., "You know Him, for He dwells with you and is in you"). Kaiser writes,

> Another example of a place where textual criticism can help us is found in John 14:17: "the Spirit of truth. The world cannot accept him, because it neither sees him nor knows him. But you know him, for he lives with you and *will be in you*" (emphasis mine). Or should we translate it as "*is in you*"? Which reading is to be preferred, *estin* or *estai*? Some early texts such as p66 and p75 read *menei . . . estai*, that is, "he abides with you and is in you." The implication of this slight difference in textual readings is enormous.[3]

The enormous implication Kaiser infers is that the indwelling of the Holy Spirit may have taken place before Jesus Christ ascended into heaven. He suggests that the reading that chooses *estai* should be preferred because it is the hardest to jell with our preconceived notions. Kaiser concludes that,

3. Kaiser, *Recovering the Bible*, loc. 769 of 4925.

indeed, the Holy Spirit indwelt believers before the resurrection and ascension of Jesus.[4] Such confidence is dubious when based on an alternate reading, no matter how robust the textual evidence is. Yet, we should not discount *the possibility* that Kaiser is correct in his conclusion.

The Great Commission presents us with one of the most explicit indications of the multipersonal understanding of God and the triune nature of God. Jesus directs that the disciples coming to faith receive baptism in the name (singular) of the Father, Son, and Holy Spirit. Once again, there is no explanation of the Holy Spirit, nor are there questions from the disciples to whom Jesus speaks in this matter. If these men knew nothing about this concept, why was there no explanation and no questions asked? I conclude that it was not entirely uncharted territory.

Traces in Acts

I must be careful using the book of Acts regarding the knowledge of the Holy Spirit before the establishment of the New Testament church. A good deal of the time frame covered by Luke happened decades after the life and ministry of Jesus when the Holy Spirit was well known to Christians. Nonetheless, the early chapters deal with a period that begins with Jesus's ascension into heaven forty days after his resurrection. The development of a mature doctrine of the Spirit by the church would generally require a much more extended period. Therefore, we may not assume that the doctrinal knowledge concerning the Holy Spirit at that time depended upon ecclesiastical progress.

Acts 1 sets before us the ascension of Christ into heaven. His last words to his apostles concern the outpouring of the Holy Spirit upon them "not many days hence" (v. 5 ASV) to the end that they will be Jesus's witnesses. Some might argue that the apostles understood nothing more than the coming of the power of God upon them. If this is so, Jesus did nothing to disabuse them of the misconception. He neither explains who the Holy Spirit is nor do the disciples ask about him.

In the same chapter (Acts 1:15–26), Luke records the naming of Matthias to replace Judas as the twelfth apostle. Peter says the prophecy "that was spoken beforehand by the Holy Spirit in the mouth of David" was necessarily fulfilled (v. 16). The language is precise: the Holy Spirit speaks with the instrumentality of David's mouth. Speaking is an activity of persons,

4. Kaiser, *Recovering the Bible*, loc. 769 of 4925.

not things! Peter said this before the descent of the Spirit promised by Jesus, so we cannot assign his knowledge of the personality of the Spirit to that occurrence. How did he know that the Holy Spirit was a person?

Acts 5 records the Lord's judgment upon Ananias and Sapphira. This judgment occurred because they lied about concealing a portion of their funds from selling their property. Peter then asked Ananias, "Why has Satan filled your heart to lie to the Holy Spirit?" (v. 3 NASB). We use this passage as one of the classic proofs of the personhood of the third person of the Trinity. Why did Peter expect Ananias to understand the question if the personhood of the Holy Spirit had been previously unknown? Remember, this circumstance took place shortly after the inauguration of the New Testament church. Why was no explanation necessary even though the Spirit's personhood made the sin most heinous?

In Acts 19, there is a passage that might appear to contradict the thesis that the Holy Spirit was known as a distinct person before New Testament times. The apostle Paul meets disciples who know only the baptism of John the Baptist. When he asks them whether they have received the baptism of the Holy Spirit, they reply, according to most translations, "We did not know there was a Holy Spirit" (v. 2). This rendering of the Greek strongly implies that there was no understanding of a personal Spirit before the onset of the apostolic teaching. I note two things in reply. First, there is no reason to believe that these disciples were Jews since Paul's ministry at this time was among the gentiles. I do not maintain the knowledge of the Holy Spirit among the non-Israelite nations before Pentecost. Second, at least one English version translates the verse in another way. The American Standard Version reads, "And they said to him, Nay. We did not so much as hear that the Holy Spirit *was given*" (Acts 19:2b, italics in the original). The phrase *was given* opens the possibility that the men were aware that the Holy Spirit existed but did not know he had been poured out upon the church. Italics denote a translator's insertion, and the ASV's translators are considered some of the most faithful to the sense of the Greek. They believed that the correct understanding required this addition to the original. This fact is something worth considering.

Conclusion

Scholars tell us that ancient Israel did not understand the doctrine of the Trinity, nor did they know that there was any diversity of persons in the divine nature. I have argued that the words that Jesus and others use in the New Testament about the Holy Spirit are inexplicable (for the most part) without assuming that those who heard them speak knew something of the Spirit and his personality.

Jesus and his apostles spoke, expecting their hearers to understand them. For example, a warning about blasphemy against a person of whom people were ignorant is no warning at all. Indeed, sometimes Jesus and Scripture speak expecting that people will ignore the message. In that case, this refusal to hear increases guilt because the audience ought to understand the message. Nevertheless, speaking in incomprehensible words does not increase accountability; instead, it provides an apparent excuse for the disobedient.

The scriptures we looked at should challenge the belief that only hints of the Trinity reveal themselves in the Old Testament. Instead, both the Holy Spirit's presence *and* the knowledge of God the Son appear in the Old Testament. For example, when Isaiah says in chapter 9 that the Son given to us shall have titles that exude divinity, what were his readers expected to think—that God would bestow upon a mere creature these titles? May it never be! Jesus said that the Old Testament scriptures testify of him. The thoughtful reader will recognize that the Scriptures testify of him as *incarnate God*. The Messiah promised in the Old Testament is a divine Messiah, and the Old Testament makes this fact known.

The attempt to remove the Messiah's deity was, in fact, the effort of the later rabbis. They wished to distance themselves from Christianity. Unbelief drove this effort, not the careful reading of the text. When Jesus pressed the meaning of Ps 110 upon the Pharisees, he insisted upon the knowledge of a divine Messiah present in the text of the Old Testament. Moreover, this was the interpretation they ought to have understood.

The triune God is eternal, and each of the three persons share this perfection. If one can believe, and the evidence for this is undeniable, that the writers of the Old Testament knew God the Son, there is no reason to doubt that God the Holy Spirit was also known by them.

Appendix B

The Unity of Israel and the Church

Introduction

This book presents the premise that the Bible is a unity that is organic rather than synthetic because the Holy Spirit intended this unity. I argue here that some scholars are in theoretical agreement with the thesis but in practice deny it. Dispensational theology does not agree with me, even in theory. This disagreement arises because dispensational theology insists that Israel and the church are entirely distinct. They say Israel consists of the physical descendants of Jacob and those gentiles giving up their gentile identity by becoming proselytes. They also say the church consists of believers whose relationship to God is solely through Christ—not the twelve patriarchs.[1]

Growing out of the separation of Israel and the church is the dispensational belief that God intended a similar divergence between the Old Testament and the (larger part) of the New Testament. In their theology, the two issues stand or fall together. The Old Testament addresses Israel, and the New Testament addresses the church. If one can show an essential unity between Israel and the church, the rupture between the Testaments ends.

1. This generalization fuzzes somewhat in practice because there is a recognition in *the church age* that gentile Christians who leave the church for non-Christian Judaism apostatize. At the same time, Jews who come to faith in Jesus Christ belong to the church. Moreover, if these Jewish Christians are alive at the "rapture," they will be taken away with all other believers, escaping the tribulation.

Appendix B

An Important Distinction

Do not read the title above as if it was "The Unity of Israel and the Gentiles." Yet, this is what I fear will take place in the minds of some when they read the title as it stands. The words *gentile* and *church* are not synonyms, nor is the latter a subset of the former. If they are synonyms, specific biblical texts have no meaning. For example, Paul rebukes Jews boasting of Jewishness while leading a hypocritical life, and he says that they cause the gentiles to blaspheme (Rom 2:24). Did Paul intend to say that such hypocritical behavior caused the church to blaspheme the name of God? Such a reading is nonsense! I do not argue that Jews are gentiles or the reverse. Instead, I argue that the church is drawn from both groups.

Gentiles and Jews, in the first century and beyond, were people groups from which God called a people for himself. God gathered those who heeded the call of the gospel into the church of Jesus Christ and separated them from the gentiles in the case of non-Jewish believers. The Bible displays this very concept in the meaning of the Greek word translated as *church*. *Ecclesia* means "the called-out ones"[2] and thus underscores the distinction between those in the church and those outside. By highlighting this distinction, the New Testament parallels the disparity between Israel and the nations[3] in the Old Testament. Therefore, we see that the Old Testament separation between Israel and the nations is a type and preparation for the distinction between the church and the unbelieving world (both Jewish and gentile) found in the New Testament economy and indeed in our times. It is a pity that, in our time, some try to emphasize differences between Israel and the church without acknowledging this typological understanding.

A Time Between the Times

A frequent source of misunderstanding comes with the failure to realize the peculiar place in redemptive history occupied by New Testament believers between the ascent of Jesus into heaven and the destruction of Herod's temple in AD 70. This era indeed was a *time between the times*. Just as an

2. Bible Hub, "1577. Ekklésia."

3. I use the word *nations* following the lead of the translators of the ESV, in which the English words *gentiles* and *gentile* do not appear in the Old Testament. The Hebrew *goyim* stands behind the English translation *nations*, while the same words are translated *ethnean* by the Greek Septuagint. The New Testament writers follow the practice of the Septuagint. See Bible Hub, "1471. Goy," and "1484. Ethnos."

overlap exists in a relay race with the baton's passing, an overlap existed when the new covenant replaced the rites and ceremonies of the old administration symbolized in the temple in Jerusalem. Because this circumstance existed, apparently separate institutions were active simultaneously. Nevertheless, this was not a permanent situation.

Moreover, there were clear signs of the old succumbing to the new. Peter declares to the household of Cornelius in Acts 10:34–37, "I most certainly understand *now* that God is not one to show partiality, but in every nation the man who fears Him and does what is right is welcome to Him. The word which He sent to the sons of Israel, preaching peace through Jesus Christ (He is Lord of all)—you yourselves know the thing which took place throughout all Judea, starting from Galilee, after the baptism which John proclaimed" (NASB).

In addition, Paul writes, "But the son of the slave was born according to the flesh, while the son of the free woman was born through promise. Now this may be interpreted allegorically: these women are two covenants. One is from Mount Sinai, bearing children for slavery; she is Hagar. Now Hagar is Mount Sinai in Arabia; she corresponds to the present Jerusalem, for she is in slavery with her children" (Gal 4:23–25 ESV).

The writer of Hebrews calls the Mosaic/Levitical economy "a shadow of the good things to come" (Heb 10:1 ESV). Nevertheless, God gave the inspired writer no prerogative to destroy the Mosaic institutions that were still intact. The Jewish Christians continued to frequent the temple as a house of prayer and to consider the Aaronic priesthood legitimate as long as it continued. However, in the back of their minds they should have had the memory of the Lord's words to them that the physical temple would be obliterated so thoroughly that no stone would remain upon another (Matt 24:2; Mark 13:2; and Luke 21:6).

The Lord does not fully explain the reason for this transition. One factor worth noting is that in the early days of the church, when it was weak and fragile, the thought that Christianity was a sect of Judaism cast a cloak of protection over the church in the eyes of Rome. The empire tolerated Judaism and therefore Christianity as a recognized religion, but the state cult viciously persecuted most other religions that challenged its authority.

The unique circumstance of *time between the times* was just that, unique! It should not be considered permanent or normative. Jesus already had offered the once-for-all sacrifice for sin, and the rites and ceremonies that pointed to that sacrifice needed to pass away. Such violently occurring destruction would have been a witness to the apostasy of those whose circumcision was merely *in the flesh*.

Two passages in the Epistle to the Romans need to be tied together. First, Rom 4:16: "For this reason it is by faith, in order that it may be in accordance with grace, so that the promise will be guaranteed to all the descendants, not only to those who are of the Law, but also to those who are of the faith of Abraham, who is the father of us all" (NASB). The next passage is Rom 9:6–8: "But it is not as though the word of God has failed. For they are not all Israel who are descended from Israel; nor are they all children because they are Abraham's descendants, but: 'through Isaac your descendants shall be named.' That is, it is not the children of the flesh who are children of God, but the children of the promise are regarded as descendants" (NASB).

The latter's reading without the former might imply that Paul was distinguishing true Jews from false Jews. However, gentile believers are included in the former since Abraham is called "the father of us all" (Rom 4:16). It is sharing the faith of Abraham—not his DNA—that makes us his offspring.

Inclusion and Expansion—Not Replacement

Dispensational theologians often cuttingly call covenant theology *replacement theology*. They believe adherents of covenant theology have stolen God's promises to Israel and appropriated them for the church. Such a viewpoint misunderstands covenant teaching. Covenantal and Reformed theology does not believe God replaced Israel. Instead, he expanded it by including believers called out from the nations. In the quotation above from Rom 9:6, Paul writes, "But it is not as though the word of God has failed." The portions of the word of God of which he speaks are those that contain God's promises to Israel. Covenant theology does not deny this fact!

The context in which we ought to view this matter is that of Matt 8:10–12: "Now when Jesus heard this, He was amazed and said to those who were following, 'Truly I say to you, I have not found such great faith with anyone in Israel. And I say to you that many will come from east and west, and recline at the table with Abraham, Isaac, and Jacob in the kingdom of heaven; but the sons of the kingdom will be thrown out into the outer darkness; in that place there will be weeping and gnashing of teeth'" (NASB).

A careful reading of the text will show that the table of which Jesus speaks is one at which Abraham, Isaac, and Jacob (whose name was Israel) are seated. The patriarchs who received the promises are sitting in the places of honor. Indeed, their presence defines the table as being in *the kingdom of heaven*. The "sons of the kingdom," who are cast out, are *false* sons. They cannot be legitimate sons because their final destination is "the outer darkness; in that place, there will be weeping and gnashing of teeth," (v. 12). This is where true sons will never go!

A continued careful reading of the text should take us further. Not all gentiles will recline at the table. Joined with the faithless "sons of the kingdom" in the darkness are all the unbelieving gentiles who also reject the gospel of Christ Jesus.

We may also ask, "For what purpose is the table laid?" Undoubtedly, the best answer is the marriage of the Lamb. Who is the bride? She is the church of Jesus Christ. We must take seriously the juxtaposition of the presence of the patriarchs at the feast that celebrates the wedding of Jesus and his church. We see expansion and inclusion here—not a replacement.

Specific New Testament Passages of Note

Romans 15:4–12

> For whatever was written in earlier times was written for our instruction, so that through perseverance and the encouragement of the Scriptures we might have hope. Now may the God who gives perseverance and encouragement grant you to be of the same mind with one another, according to Christ Jesus, so that with one purpose and one voice you may glorify the God and Father of our Lord Jesus Christ. Therefore, accept one another, just as Christ also accepted us, for the glory of God. For I say that Christ has become a servant to the circumcision in behalf of the truth of God, to confirm the promises given to the fathers, and for the Gentiles to glorify God for His mercy; as it is written: "Therefore I will give praise to You among the Gentiles, And I will sing praises to Your name." Again he says, "Rejoice, you Gentiles, with His people." And again, "Praise the Lord all you Gentiles, And let all the peoples praise Him." Again Isaiah says, "There shall come the root of Jesse, And He who arises to rule over the Gentiles, In Him will the Gentiles hope." (NASB)

Remember, as we look at these verses, when Paul wrote to the Romans, he wrote to a church drawn from both Jews and gentiles. Unless he specifically addressed one segment of the church, what he said, he said for the sake of all. Therefore, when in verse 4 he wrote, "Whatever was written in earlier times was written for our instruction," he included all in the congregation in the usefulness of the writings of the Old Testament. The instruction is for the entire congregation of Rome and, by extension, the whole New Testament church.

Noteworthy is the fact that Paul's statement concerns the reason for the writing. That written in earlier epochs was written "for our instruction." This concept is quite different from taking texts intended for purposes in previous eras and using them for other purposes later. Paul connected the writings in the past with their usefulness in his day, and he said this was intended.

It is essential to see the usefulness of the writings stretching back to the purpose for which the writers set them down. It was, said Paul, "so that through perseverance and the encouragement of the Scriptures we might have hope" (v. 4). If there is no unity between Israel and the church, what hope could a church derive from writings intended for an entirely different group of people? Paul's language ties these ancient scriptures to the church's hope through perseverance in them and encouragement by them.

The mention of perseverance and encouragement led Paul to set forth God as the giver of these two possessions. Paul hoped that these two qualities would produce *agreement* in the Roman church. The text shows that the agreeing parties are to be Roman Christians drawn respectively from the Jews and gentiles. The end to which the apostle saw this agreement tending, he described in these words: "So that with one purpose and one voice you may glorify the God and Father of our Lord Jesus Christ" (v. 6).

Up to this point, this passage of Romans had tied together both Jewish and gentile Christians based on Old Testament scriptures that supplied perseverance and encouragement as God's gifts to these people. The result was the worship of the Father, through the Son, and (presumably) the Holy Spirit. Moreover, Paul *gave* an imperative resulting from these truths. Jews and gentiles in the Roman church were to accept one another. The acceptance was established upon the approval of both groups within the church by Jesus Christ. Of Jews, Paul wrote, "For I say that Christ has become a servant to the circumcision in behalf of the truth of God, to confirm the promises given to the fathers" (v. 8). The confirmation of the promises *to the fathers*, thus, has its fulfillment in the arena of the church, and it parallels God's plan for the gentiles.

God's plan for the gentiles received emphasis in the conclusion of Paul's argument here. I quote him once more:

> . . . and for the Gentiles to glorify God for His mercy; as it is written: "Therefore I will give praise to You among the Gentiles, And I will sing praises to Your name." Again he says, "Rejoice, you Gentiles, with His people." And again, "Praise the Lord all you Gentiles, And let all the peoples praise Him." Again Isaiah says, "There shall come the root of Jesse, And He who arises to rule over the Gentiles, In Him will the Gentiles hope." (vv. 9–12)

Paul said all this hung upon "whatever was written in earlier times" (v. 4). Jews and gentiles were inextricably mixed as they formed the components of the one church of Jesus Christ. Surely, what was relevant to the church of the first century is relevant to the church of the twenty-first century.

One cannot argue that this passage has nothing to do with Israel and speaks only to Jews in the church age. Paul's language was unmistakable in references that can only be to Israel. Jesus, he said, was a servant to "the *circumcision*," and he performed his service to "*confirm the promises to the fathers*" (v. 8).

1 Corinthians 5:1

> It is actually reported that there is sexual immorality among you, and sexual immorality of such a kind *as does not exist even among the Gentiles*, namely, that someone has his father's wife. (NASB, emphasis mine)

Though brief, the phrase emphasized in the quotation above speaks volumes concerning the unity of Israel and the church. Corinth was a church drawn almost exclusively from the gentiles, yet Paul contrasts the abominable scandal in the church with the practices among the gentiles. The world of Paul's day knew of two classifications, Israel and the gentiles. If the Corinthian believers were not gentiles, how could we separate them from Israel?

Some would say that the church is a third category, not gentiles and not Israel. This observation is valid if one substitutes the word *Jew* for *Israel* in the statement above. The two terms are not identical, even in the Old

Testament context. The New Testament knows nothing of a "true people of God" whose circumcision is merely outward, who turn their backs upon Jesus Christ, and who persecute the church. However, the New Testament does know of those who are of the so called synagogue of Satan.

Ephesians 2:11–22

> Therefore remember that *formerly* you, the Gentiles in the flesh, who are called "Uncircumcision" by the so-called "Circumcision," which is performed in the flesh by human hands—remember that you were **at that time separated from Christ, excluded from the commonwealth of Israel**, and **strangers** to the covenants of promise, having no hope and without God in the world. But now in Christ Jesus you who **formerly** *were far off* have been *brought near* by the blood of Christ. For He Himself is our peace, who **made both *groups into one* and broke down the barrier of the dividing wall** by **abolishing** in His flesh **the enmity** which is in the law of commandments contained in ordinances, so that in himself he might make **the two into one new man** thus establishing peace and might **reconcile** them both *in one body* to God through the cross by its **having put to death the enmity**. And he came and preached peace to you who were far away and peace to those who were near; For through him we both have our **access in one Spirit to the Father**. So then you are no longer strangers and aliens but you are fellow citizens with the saints and are of God's household, having been built on the foundation of the apostles and prophets, Christ Jesus Himself being the cornerstone, in whom **the whole building being fitted together**, is growing into a holy temple in the Lord, in whom you also are being built together into a dwelling of God in the Spirit. (NASB)[4]

There is probably no passage of Scripture in the Bible that displays the unity of Israel and the church more explicitly. The apostle begins by showing the previously existing hostility between Israel and the nations. He contrasts that situation with what has come about because of the work of Jesus Christ, which has brought about a unity that he describes in the most emphatic language.

We note that before Paul dealt with the real disjunction of Israel and the gentiles in the past, he spoke of one that continues in the unbelieving

4. Italics are in the original, bold is my emphasis.

world. This disjunction is the distinction between uncircumcision and circumcision of a fleshly sort. Paul's method of talking about circumcision leads us to understand that the name calling they exercised had no sanction from God, for this took place in their present experience.

The past, however, was different. There was a time when the negative view of the gentiles had God's approval. It is not a reference to the contempt unbelieving Jews were heaping upon gentiles in the first century, whether Christian or not. Paul referred to the time when *God* poured his wrath on the gentiles. They were "separate from Christ, excluded from the commonwealth of Israel, and strangers to the covenants of promise, having no hope and without God in the world" (v. 12).

"But now," said Paul, something happened. Christ has dealt with all these real and terrifying demerits through his work. The almost infinite difference between Israel and the gentiles God has overcome in Christ. The hostility that at one time existed and existed rightly (on Israel's part) had its end in the cross and the blood of Jesus.

Yet, we ask, what exactly did the cross accomplish regarding removing the hostility? Through the cross, Jesus has given both one access to the Father, made the two groups one, broken down the barrier between them, and brought a reconciliation that presents them in one body to God.

What was the result of these accomplishments of Christ's atonement? It was building a new kind of temple of God for his spiritual worship. This temple is built—not from stone and mortar but from believers drawn from Israel and the gentiles.

We must remember everything that Paul said here he based on the distinction between then and now. And one of the things that separated the two groups was that gentiles were "excluded from the commonwealth of Israel." If that separation still exists, then the work of Jesus Christ did not accomplish what Paul said it did.

Therefore, these verses provide a message of unity of Israel and the church. The cross is not the alternate way of salvation for those not blessed enough to be covered by membership in the people of Israel. Jesus calls to himself "those who [are] near" and "those who [are] far away" (v. 17), and he does so by one means and one means only, the blood of the cross. The temple that the Holy Spirit constructs is not a temporary building, and the idea that the temple God builds from the new humanity will be replaced by rebuilding a Jewish temple of stone and mortar is repugnant to the sense of Paul's argument here.

Appendix B

Conclusion

I have not attempted to give a critique of the whole of dispensational theology and hermeneutics. Instead, I am interested in presenting the unity of Israel and the church. When one presents them as separate institutions composed of distinct people groups looking to a different set of promises that have different ways of fulfillment, the unity of God's word is severely compromised.

Still more dangerous is that Christ himself is divided under that set of circumstances, and he fills one function for the worship and service of the church, but he provides a different position for Israel. It is even the case that the ascription of the title Christ for the Savior of the church is anachronistic, for that is the title he holds as Israel's promised ruler.

For these reasons, we must understand that there are not two distinct peoples of God, and Jesus Christ does not have two brides. The "blessed hope" of Christ's return is one hope that brings all his promises consummation for all his redeemed, and judgment to those who scorn his sacrifice. Peter, an apostle of the newly instituted *New Testament* church, declared "that God has made Him both Lord and Christ—this Jesus whom you crucified" (Acts 2:36).

Bibliography

Aland, Kurt, et al., eds., *The Greek New Testament*. 3rd ed., corrected. Stuttgart: United Bible Societies, 1983.

Allis, Oswald T. *The Five Books of Moses: A Reexamination of the Modern Theory That the Pentateuch Is a Late Compilation from Diverse and Conflicting Sources by Authors and Editors Whose Identity Is Completely Unknown*. Phillipsburg, NJ: P&R, 1974.

Augustine. *Quaestiones in Heptateuchum*. Patrologia Latina, edited by J.-P. Migne, 34:623. Paris: Garnier, 1861.

Berkhof, Louis. *Principles of Biblical Interpretation*. Grand Rapids: Baker, 1950.

Bible Hub. "314. Acharon." https://biblehub.com/hebrew/314.htm.

———. "1350. Gaal." https://biblehub.com/hebrew/1350.htm.

———. "1352. Goel." https://biblehub.com/hebrew/1352.htm.

———. "1471. Goy." https://biblehub.com/hebrew/1471.htm.

———. "1484. Ethnos." https://biblehub.com/greek/1484.htm.

———. "1577. Ekklésia." https://biblehub.com/greek/1577.htm.

———. "1752. Heneka." https://biblehub.com/greek/1752.htm.

———. "2435. Hilastérion." https://biblehub.com/greek/2435.htm.

———. "2532. Kai." https://biblehub.com/greek/2532.htm.

———. "2623. Chasid." https://biblehub.com/hebrew/2623.htm.

———. "3004. Legó." https://biblehub.com/greek/3004.htm.

———. "3427. Yashab." https://biblehub.com/hebrew/3427.htm.

———. "3651. Ken." https://biblehub.com/hebrew/3651.htm.

———. "3741. Hosios." https://biblehub.com/greek/3741.htm.

———. "3825. Palin." https://biblehub.com/greek/3825.htm.

———. "3850. Parabole." https://biblehub.com/greek/3850.htm.

———. "4277." https://biblehub.com/greek/4277.htm.

———. "4428. Melek." https://biblehub.com/hebrew/4428.htm.

———. "4771. Su." https://biblehub.com/greek/4771.htm.

———. "5179. Tupos." https://biblehub.com/greek/5179.htm.

———. "5228. Huper." https://biblehub.com/greek/5228.htm.

———. "5258. Nacak." https://biblehub.com/hebrew/5258.htm.

———. "5921. Al." https://biblehub.com/hebrew/5921.htm.

———. "6083. Aphar." https://biblehub.com/hebrew/6083.htm.

———. "6965. Qum." https://biblehub.com/hebrew/6965.htm.

Bray, Gerald Lewis. *Holiness and the Will of God: Perspectives on the Theology of Tertullian*. London: Marshall, Morgan & Scott, 1979.

Bibliography

Brown, Francis, et al. *A Hebrew and English Lexicon of the Old Testament*. Oxford: Clarendon Press, 1906.

Calvin, John. *Commentary on the Epistle to the Romans*. Translated and edited by John Owen. Edinburgh: Calvin Translation Society, 1849.

Collins, C. John. Study notes for Psalms in the *ESV Study Bible*, edited by Wayne Grudem et al. Wheaton, IL: Crossway, 2008. Kindle.

Doyle, Arthur Conan. *The Sign of the Four*. London: Penguin Classics, 2014.

Elam, Andrew M., et al. *Merit and Moses: A Critique of the Klinean Doctrine of Republication*. Eugene, OR: Wipf and Stock, 2014.

Enns, Peter. "Apostolic Hermeneutics and an Evangelical Doctrine of Scripture: Moving Beyond a Modernist Impasse." *Westminster Theological Journal* 65 (2003) 263–87.

Estelle, Bryan D., et al., eds. *The Law Is Not of Faith: Essays on Works and Grace in the Mosaic Covenant*. Phillipsburg, NJ: P&R, 2009.

Fairbairn, Donald. "Patristic Exegesis and Theology: The Cart and the Horse." *Westminster Theological Journal* 69 (2007) 1–19.

Fairbairn, Patrick. *The Typology of Scripture: Viewed in Connection with the Whole Series of the Divine Dispensations*. Vol. 1. 1900. Repr., Grand Rapids: Baker, 1951.

Firth, David G., and Paul D. Wegner, eds. *Presence, Power, and Promise: The Role of the Spirit of God in the Old Testament*. Nottingham, UK: Apollos, 2011.

Hendriksen, William. *New Testament Commentary: Exposition of the Gospel of Matthew*. Grand Rapids: Baker, 1973.

Herrick, Greg. "The Use of Psalm 16:8–11 in Acts 2:25–28." Bible.org, July 4, 2004. https://bible.org/article/use-psalm-168-11-acts-225-28.

Hill, Andrew E., and John H. Walton. *A Survey of the Old Testament*. Grand Rapids: Zondervan, 2003.

Horne, George. *Commentary on the Psalms*. 1825. Repr., Audubon, NJ: Old Paths, 1977.

Jamieson, Robert, et al. *A Commentary Critical and Explanatory on the Whole Bible*. Grand Rapids: Eerdmans, 1945.

Johnson, Dennis E. *Walking with Jesus Through His Word: Discovering Christ in All the Scriptures*. Phillipsburg, NJ: P&R, 2015.

Kaiser, Walter C., Jr. *Recovering the Unity of the Bible: One Continuous Story, Plan, and Purpose*. Grand Rapids: Zondervan, 2009. Kindle.

Keil, Carl Friedrich, and Franz Delitzsch. *Psalms*. Vol. 5 of *Biblical Commentary on the Old Testament*, translated by James Martin et al. Grand Rapids: Eerdmans, 1973.

McEwen, William. *The Glory and Fullness of Jesus Christ: In the Most Remarkable Types, Figures, and Allegories of the Old Testament*. Edited by Gordon J. Keddie. Grand Rapids: Reformation Heritage, 2022.

Mill, William Hodge, ed. *Essays on the Church by Members of the University of Oxford*. Oxford: Parker, 1839.

Nicoll, William R. "Commentary on Habakkuk 2." The Expositor's Bible Commentary. StudyLight.org. https://www.studylight.org/commentaries/eng/teb/habakkuk-2.html.

Owen, John. *The Holy Spirit*. Vol. 3 of *The Works of John Owen*, edited by William H. Goold. Carlisle, PA: Banner of Truth Trust, 1965.

Oxford English Dictionary. "Deus ex machina." December 2024. Kindle.

Payne, J. Barton. *Encyclopedia of Biblical Prophecy: The Complete Guide to Scriptural Predictions and Their Fulfillment*. New York: Harper & Row, 1973.

Selvaggio, Anthony T. *From Bondage to Liberty: The Gospel According to Moses.* Phillipsburg, NJ: P&R, 2004.

Shakespeare, William. *Julius Caesar.* Edited by Barbara Mowat et al. Washington, DC: Folger Shakespeare Library, n.d.

Stoppard, Tom. *Rosencrantz and Guildenstern Are Dead.* London: Faber & Faber, 1967.

Tertullian. *Apology.* Translated by S. Thelwall. Logos Virtual Libary. http://www.logoslibrary.org/tertullian/apology/index.html.

Thornwell, James H. *Theological and Controversial.* Vol. 3 of *The Collected Writings of James Henley Thornwell*, edited by John L. Girardeau and John B. Adger. 1873. Repr., Edinburgh: Banner of Truth Trust, 1986.

The Westminster Standards. Larger Catechism. https://thewestminsterstandard.org/westminster-larger-catechism/.

———. Shorter Catechism. https://thewestminsterstandard.org/westminster-shorter-catechism/.

———. The Westminster Confession of Faith. https://thewestminsterstandard.org/the-westminster-confession/.

Wingard, Brian T. "'As the Lord Puts Words in Her Mouth': The Supremacy of Scripture in the Ecclesiology of James Henley Thornwell and Its Influence on the Presbyterian Churches of the South." PhD diss., Westminster Theological Seminary, 1992.

Young, Edward J. *The Book of Isaiah: The English Text, with Introduction, Exposition, and Notes.* 3 vols. Grand Rapids: Eerdmans, 1992.

———. *Thy Word Is Truth.* 1957. Repr., Grand Rapids: Eerdmans, 1981.

www.ingramcontent.com/pod-product-compliance
Lightning Source LLC
LaVergne TN
LVHW050639100826
845148LV00011B/1910

* 9 7 9 8 3 8 5 2 5 6 9 0 7 *